St. Hildegard's Garden

Paul Ferris

St. Hildegard's Garden

Recipes and Remedies for Healing Body and Soul

Hildegard of Bingen's Illustrated Herbarium

Translated by James Henri McMurtrie and Hunter McClure

SOPHIA INSTITUTE PRESS

Manchester, New Hampshire

Copyright © 2024 by Groupe Elidia Éditions du Rocher, 28, rue Comte Félix-Gastaldi — BP 521 — 98 015 Monaco

English translation copyright © by Sophia Institute Press

First published in French as *L'herbarium illustré d'Hildegarde de Bingen* © 2024 by Groupe Elidia Éditions du Rocher.

Printed in the United States of America. All rights reserved.

Cover by Emma Helstrom

Cover image: *Stylish collection of red ribbon banners (1002073247), image derived from ELENA AI / stock.adobe.com; Hildegard of Bingen (1647836983), image derived from Natata / shutterstock.com.*

Sophia Institute Press
Box 5284, Manchester, NH 03108
1-800-888-9344
www.SophiaInstitute.com

Sophia Institute Press is a registered trademark of Sophia Institute.

Hardcover ISBN 979-8-88911-372-0

ebook ISBN 979-8-88911-374-4

Library of Congress Control Number: 2025934981

5th printing

Table of Contents

FOREWORD

This beautiful book opens a door to a hidden realm, a time and place in history permeated with and characterized by Christian faith. With its lovely images of some of the plants St. Hildegard loved and her descriptions of their virtues, we enter the garden of a world different from ours.

It's the realm of St. Hildegard of Bingen, Benedictine nun. She was the medieval *mulier fortis* (strong woman); the mystical—and mysterious—exemplar of a world obscured in our imaginations as a result of the burden of the Enlightenment, for which "the Dark Ages" represent superstition and bondage.

To approach St. Hildegard, we need to learn to overcome this contempt, the defect of a culture that suffers from what C.S. Lewis called chronological snobbery, "the uncritical acceptance of the intellectual climate common to our own age and the assumption that whatever has gone out of date is on that account discredited."[1] This condition leads us, perhaps, to think we stand uniquely outside the conditioning of history—that we are not, as all others before us were, "products of our time." Perhaps other generations also had this bias, but they didn't have our fatal hubris: unreflective dismissal of past wisdom.

Before the rationalism of Descartes, the thought of inventing culture anew didn't occur to people, nor did they feel a sense of alienation from the rest of the created world. Culture was passed down by means of respect and a sense of duty to preserve known things. In this disconnected state, however, the heavens became "space"—cold and distant. Finally, we arrived at a point of defining ourselves by rejecting tradition—a putatively flexible stance that itself, ironically, becomes traditional. In that way, an undetectable hardening of the structure of our collective mind occurs.

1 *Surprised by Joy*, chap. 13.

It isn't easy to recover from the situation in which we find ourselves: a state of presumed superiority but also of misery, the misery of sensing how cut off we are from what we cannot help desiring, which is, in fact, connectedness — to the past and to the cosmos.

There are three main obstacles we face in appreciating St. Hildegard fully, and all of them produce our alienation from the medieval world. The first obstacle is our insistence on science as pseudo-religion; the second, the rigid dogma imposed by feminism; the third, a narrow idea of orthodoxy.

We don't know much about St. Hildegard; what we do know is undeniably fascinating. Her wildness, her ecstatic vision, her achievement, and the sheer scope of her inquiry we reflexively assume are *opposed* to the age she lived in and more suitable to ours. The opposite is the case. It is our world that has only one mode: materialism. Ours is the one that regards with suspicion whatever has not first passed through the analytics of the experts.

Hildegard's imaginative faculty and her closeness to the spiritual realm seem in *opposition* to our material, scientific view and inferior to it as not being, above all, concerned with measurement and analysis. We consider the unseen of dubious reality. We tend to view things as products of random forces emerging from and resulting in conflict. Even when he has faith in God, modern man almost can't help being swayed by the materialistic scientism, rooted in Kantian relativism, that wants to describe our perception upon inhaling the celestial fragrance of freshly gathered goldenrod in reductive terms.

In contrast, Hildegard (very much in keeping with her context) revels in the encounter with everything she surveys, all of it transmitted by a beneficent, transcendent entity, oriented to unity (with the exception of the evil spirits, also much more real to her than to us). She considers the healing power of a plant a reality to be discovered, used, and revered — but not worshipped.

If we can suspend the temptation to assume that *our* way of knowing the created world is the *only* way, we will have a better chance of understanding the material explanation as just that: one explanation — useful but not decisive. The temptation is toward a conviction that the senses are not a means of knowing but rather an impression emanating from the subject doing the sensing. For Hildegard, and in the medieval model, the conviction of the unity of life and the cosmos means accepting the palpable goodness of an herb's scent as part of a whole and compatible with it and its meaning, not in opposition or conflict. She says, "The juice of the fern, created for wisdom, is part of what is good in wisdom and nature, a sign of goodness and holiness."

When she identifies a plant with a sign or as a part of some invisible virtue, it seems so foreign to us, or perhaps a quirky affectation. In the medieval world, people tried to fit every sort of thing into one coherent, intricate, unified model, arranged according to its position in relation, ultimately, to God; without a doubt, Hildegard was speaking the language of her milieu. In the past few years, even we have experienced the cracks in a rigid scientism, in that almost religious faith in the industrialization of medicine. Perhaps there is a longing for a new—yet also ancient—recovery of the hierarchy of being and nature's place in it, ordered to our well-being.

Our second difficulty with arriving at an organic understanding of Hildegard—her world, her thought, and her motivations—is the dichotomy imposed by feminism. For medieval man, and certainly for Hildegard, the universe is characterized by hierarchy, not equality. The feminist, however, cannot grasp a paradigm of complementarity without defaulting to a binary and indeed positive-negative connotation. The feminist wants to force Hildegard into this model, stamping her with obligatory traits of resistance, discord, and strife.

Like every person's life since the Fall of Adam, Hildegard's life involved struggle and suffering: physical, spiritual, and mental. She had visions she kept secret at first and then expressed in her music and her art. She was a daughter of St. Benedict and formed by his Rule from the time, as a child, she entered the convent. She implicitly accepted, for instance, the idea that chant, a particular accomplishment of hers, is the music of worship, descending on man from a primordial and sacred sphere. As a Benedictine, she was patterned according to the mind of her founder, when, in his Rule, he instructs his monks to pray according to Psalm 138:1: "In the presence of the angels I will sing to you."

In his commemorative sermon "The Regensburg Tradition and the Reform of the Liturgy," then-Cardinal Ratzinger says, "But one fact is of fundamental importance: the sacred liturgy is not something which the monks manufacture or produce. It exists before they were there; it is an entering into heavenly liturgy which was already taking place."[2] For the twenty-first century, chant is reduced to one genre of music among

---

2   Cardinal Joseph Ratzinger, "In the Presence of the Angels I Will Sing Your Praise," *Adoremus Bulletin*, December 15, 1996, https://adoremus.org/1996/12/cardinal-ratzinger-in-the-presence-of-the-angels-i-will-sing-your-praise/.

many. For a Benedictine of the sixth century (and for Christians everywhere until recently), not so; its origins are in the mists of divine bestowal. Chanting the Office formed Hildegard. That experience, so far from ours, brought forth new forms of her own making.

She understood ailments of all kinds and knew—and recorded—remedies for them. She was a healer and also a philosopher-theologian. She captured the elusive life-giving quality that permeates all of God's creation and has its source in Him, giving it the inspired name *viriditas*—greenness, vigor, "growing upwards towards the light," as the very Victorian Anthony Trollope would put it in his own, dry fashion.[3] Not having any binary view of "ecology" as a category separate from creation as a whole, Hildegard meant *viriditas* to be a principle of life and growth, not a political statement.

She seems to have had a choleric temperament. Certainly, her stubbornness stood her well in carrying out her principles and discharging her authority. Her many letters demonstrate her spiritedness, her freedom, and her conviction. As abbess, her leadership was affirmed, accepted, and ratified *by Church and state.* She had confidence in addressing the highest authorities above her as well as those for whom she was responsible. Those same letters received responses that demonstrate the respect that emperors, popes, bishops, priests, and saints all had for her. Their deference to her character, position, and causes (whatever they happened to be, and they were many) give the lie to the feminist paradigm of a power struggle. To the modern mind, elaborate reiteration of rank can seem antagonistic or rebuking; to one accustomed to hierarchical society, it is simply a ratification of form, a ritual of sorts; it is no affirmation of feminist theory.

We will not understand Hildegard by putting her in opposition to her world; nor can we pit her against men and hope to see things the way she did. She stood out in her time, and that in itself is simply what it is. As Pope Benedict said in his proclamation making her a Doctor of the Church, "At the invitation first of Hadrian IV and later of Alexander III, Hildegard practised a fruitful apostolate, something unusual for a woman at that time, making several journeys, not without hardship and difficulty, to preach even in public squares and in various cathedral churches, such as at Cologne, Trier, Liège, Mainz, Metz, Bamberg and Würzburg."[4]

---

3 Anthony Trollope, *Can You Forgive Her?*, chap. 21.

4 Apostolic letter proclaiming Saint Hildegard of Bingen, professed nun of the Order of Saint Benedict, a Doctor of the Universal Church (October 7, 2012), no. 2, https://www.vatican.va/content/benedict-xvi/en/apost_letters/documents/hf_ben-xvi_apl_20121007_ildegarda-bingen.html.

It was unusual for a woman of her time because it was unusual, period. It's easy to miss or gloss over that "at the invitation of" and imagine she did such feats in *defiance* of male authority. From that error comes the casting of St. Hildegard as a feminist icon.

To say something like "Saint Hildegard of Bingen was a pioneering figure in the history of feminism,"[5] a sentiment found throughout popular as well as academic treatments of her, is to impose a category that did not exist. Extracting ourselves from this solipsism is made more difficult by the evident feminism of her biographers. Their bias casts its shadow on their interpretation of her works, and this, in turn, colors all secondary sketches.

St. Hildegard is, above all, a woman of faith in God, in the mysteries of revelation. When Pope Benedict XVI made her a Doctor of the Church, he emphasized:

> This great woman truly stands out crystal clear against the horizon of history for her holiness of life and the originality of her teaching. And, as with every authentic human and theological experience, her authority reaches far beyond the confines of a single epoch or society; despite the distance of time and culture, her thought has proven to be of lasting relevance. . . .
>
> Hildegard's teaching is considered eminent both for its depth, the correctness of its interpretation, and the originality of its views. The texts she produced are refreshing in their authentic "intellectual charity" and emphasize the power of penetration and comprehensiveness of her contemplation of the mystery of the Blessed Trinity, the Incarnation, the Church, humanity and nature as God's creation, to be appreciated and respected.[6]

St. John Henry Newman said, "It is his [Satan's] policy to split us up and divide us, to dislodge us gradually from off our rock of strength." We miss knowing Hildegard if we insist that a woman is either a compliant victim or a dynamic rebel. We see everything

---

5   3aint, "How Has Hildegard of Bingen's Work Been Embraced by Feminists?," Saint Hildegard von Bingen, accessed February 19, 2025, https://sainthildegard.com/how-has-hildegard-work-been-embraced-by-feminists/.

6   Apostolic letter proclaiming Saint Hildegard, nos. 1, 3.

in terms of conflict. Harmony has no meaning for us, and beauty is lost in subjectivism. The transcendentals are consigned as artifacts in a museum of quaint thoughts.

Instead, St. Hildegard, like many great souls throughout history, lived on an intense plane. She wholly embraced every doctrine of the Church, as her writings and those of her contemporaries show. Despite her rather impressive credential of being a Doctor of the Church, we sometimes encounter a third misapprehension about her, that she was somehow not orthodox or that she took some aspect of the Faith to remake in her own image.

I wonder if that idea has come about because of her unusual poetic and dramatic narration of her visions, in which she expresses God's point of view. I can imagine the unsuspecting reader dipping into her works and, without grasping the context, coming away with the idea that she thought *herself* God. In her *Book of Divine Works*, Hildegard writes in this voice, envisioning Caritas, the spirit (the Holy Spirit) of Divine Love:

> I am the supreme and fiery force who sets all living sparks alight and breathes forth no mortal things, but judges them as they are. Circling above the circumscribing circle with my superior wings, which is to say circling with wisdom, I have ordered the cosmos rightly.

In his apostolic letter proclaiming her a Doctor of the universal Church, Pope Benedict said:

> The teaching of the holy Benedictine nun stands as a beacon for *homo viator*. Her message appears extraordinarily timely in today's world, which is especially sensitive to the values that she proposed and lived. For example, we think of Hildegard's charismatic and speculative capacity, which offers a lively incentive to theological research; her reflection on the mystery of Christ, considered in its beauty; the dialogue of the Church and theology with culture, science and contemporary art; the ideal of the consecrated life as a possibility for human fulfilment; her appreciation of the liturgy as a celebration of life; her understanding of the reform of the Church, not as an empty change of structure but

as conversion of heart; her sensitivity to nature, whose laws are to be safeguarded and not violated.[7]

Hildegard did not think she was part of the Trinity; she did not posit some New Age pseudo-religion. She was a shining beacon, lit from within by God and lighting the path to Him.

We perhaps could all benefit from the advice given in a letter to Eleanor of Aquitaine, in which the wise Hildegard told that monarch:

> Your mind is like a wall battered by a storm. You look all around, and you find no rest. Stay calm, and stand firm, relying on God and your fellow creatures, and God will aid you in all your tribulations.
>
> May God give you His blessing and His help in all your works.[8]

As you turn the pages of *St. Hildegard's Garden*, my prayer is that you will be drawn to a greater appreciation of St. Hildegard, a great and holy woman.

Leila Marie Lawler
March 7, 2025
Feast of St. Thomas Aquinas, Confessor and Doctor of the Church

---

7   Apostolic letter proclaiming Saint Hildegard, no. 7.

8   Joseph L. Baird, *The Personal Correspondence of Hildegard of Bingen* (New York: Oxford University Press, 2006).

Preface:
Guided by St. Hildegard

Welcome to Hildegard's garden! A garden that is beautiful and practical, inventive and organized, delightful and ecological. Whether square, rectangular, or circular, this garden can be cultivated on a small patch of land. But it can also be planted in a corner of your mind or heart. This is the spirit of this book in which Hildegard's favorite plants are described in her own words. It is astonishing that Hildegard was able to gather so much knowledge in such a tumultuous time, and it remains inspiring that her advice on plants is still relevant today.

☙ Understanding Hildegard Through the Knowledge of Her Time

To live and eat according to Hildegard's recommendations, using only the plants she describes, would mean eliminating most fruits and vegetables from our tables. These fruits and vegetables neither looked, tasted, nor felt the same in her time. Indeed, Hildegard had little appreciation for carrots, turnips, or even pears. Today, we are fortunate to have fruits and vegetables that are much tastier and more nutritious than those of the Middle Ages. Over several generations, horticulture and fruit cultivation have made remarkable progress. We are also lucky to enjoy tomatoes, potatoes, pumpkins, and avocados, which were introduced to Europe following Christopher Columbus's discovery of the Americas.

Some of Hildegard's countless recommendations are no longer applicable simply because researchers have been unable to identify certain plant species she mentioned. However, despite the nine centuries that separate her from us, the majority of her advice remains relevant. As a pioneer of European phytotherapy, she cataloged and described hundreds of ingredients from plant, mineral, and animal origins. Her recipes, remedies, nutritional advice, and holistic view of the human being are still valuable today.

This book aims to remain faithful to Hildegard's thought while being practical for everyday use.

More Than Just Health Recipes

The description of a plant can become a true poem. For instance, when Hildegard speaks of the apple tree, she notes: "At the moment its leaves begin to unfurl in spring, they are tender and healthy, like young girls before they bring a child into the world." For Hildegard, plants, animals, minerals, the earth, dew, and the seasons are all interconnected: everything exists in harmony within a harmonious world. She offers us the means to restore this marvelous balance.

Through her knowledge of diverse creatures, Hildegard dedicated her life to others. Our illnesses, she observed, are often caused by our disrespect for nature and our own bodies. Hildegard explored the knowledge available in her time, conducted experiments, prayed, and cataloged ingredients to heal both soul and body. She created health remedies, cantatas, prayers, and even an entirely new language.

The Marketing of Simple Medicinal Plants Is Not Simple

Today, simple medicinal plants fall under various regulatory categories, making them not always easy to obtain. Legislation—whether national or EU-wide—is highly complex. It distinguishes between edible plants, condiment plants, plants classified as dietary supplements, and plants considered medicinal substances that only doctors or pharmacists are authorized to prescribe. A list compiled by health authorities identifies approximately two hundred varieties as toxic. Among these are several plants recommended by Hildegard. Strict adherence to this list would render any work on Hildegard's remedies incomplete and historically inaccurate.

Together with the publisher, we have chosen to include certain plants valued by Hildegard, even if they are highly regulated for administrative reasons. These include boxwood, lungwort, and fern—plants commonly found in nature and traditionally used, yet dangerous in high doses. For each, I have noted its toxicity and any potential side effects.

❧ Staying True to Hildegard's Words

It is essential to remain as faithful as possible to Hildegard's writings, even though she did not specify dosages and some plants remain unidentified. The terminology she used can sometimes be vague or applicable to multiple species. For some plants, multiple interpretations are possible. Consequently, I sometimes make choices that differ from those of other authors or translators. For instance, when Hildegard speaks of a thistle and emphasizes its "spines," the milk thistle (*Silybum marianum*) seems the most obvious candidate. However, I choose the blessed thistle (*Centaurea benedicta*), whose spines are even more formidable and whose uses align better with Hildegard's descriptions.

❧ Hildegard Guides Us

One senses that in Hildegard's writings there is more than just knowledge of plants; without a doubt, these "diverse creatures" are connected to a world that eludes our grasp.

Paul Ferris

St. Hildegard's Garden

PART 1

An Extraordinary Life,
A Divine Work

Hildegard was born in 1098 in Bermersheim, in the Palatinate region, which roughly corresponds to today's Rhineland. The tenth child of a family of minor nobility, she was destined to enter religious life. From a very young age, she experienced visions. "At the age of three," she wrote, "I saw a light so intense that my soul was shaken, but because of my youth, I could not speak of it."

❧ Painful Visions

While in the company of her nurse, she noticed a cow and described it: "Look at the lovely little calf in that cow. It is white with spots on its forehead, its feet, and its back." The nurse recounted the child's comment to Hildegard's parents. When the calf was born, everyone witnessed the accuracy of her prediction.

Hildegard feared unsettling those around her. She began speaking less and less about her visions, which were sometimes marvelous, sometimes terrifying, and only describable as "images" — vivid, colorful, and compelling. Her parents

Hildegard receives images, visions sent from Heaven.

decided that at the age of eight, she was old enough to learn to read, write, and sing psalms. She was sent to a nearby monastery, where Jutta, a nun six years her senior, took her under her wing. A deep friendship developed between the young nun and the child. At last, Hildegard found someone she could confide in. She shared with Jutta the "images" that consumed her—obsessive and incomprehensible visions.

Several decades later, Hildegard would recount these "images," sometimes wondrous, sometimes terrifying.

✺ A Studious Life Dedicated to Spreading Her Visions

Jutta died in 1136. Hildegard was extremely sad. She no longer had a friend to confide in. The same year, she was elected abbess of Disibodenberg. She continued to be tormented by her visions. Soon, voices drove her to reveal these "images" she was always complaining about. But she resisted doing this as much as she could.

> "Behold, in the forty-fourth year of my temporal race, while I was very fearfully attaching myself to a celestial vision, I trembled greatly and saw a very big luster in which a voice was heard from Heaven. It was telling me: 'Fragile human being, ashes from ashes, rot from rot, say and write what you see and hear.'"

Finally, Brother Volmar, who was her confessor, ordered her to transcribe these visions. Bernard of Clairvaux, whose advice she sought, confirmed that she must do so. A copy of her writings was shown to a bishop and then to others during the Synod of Trèves in 1147, and, finally, to the pope. Of course, the witch hunts had not yet been set up. The Inquisition began only a century later—in 1233—with Gregory IX's publication of the papal bull *Vox in Rama*. However, the Church, which was facing many heresies and false prophets, wanted to avoid all mystification, fraud, and risk of distraction. Hildegard was questioned by a committee of theologians. They confirmed that Hildegard was not delusional and did not lie—and that her visions. did not contradict the Church's dogma. Her visions were recognized as authentic.

Later, Hildegard wrote *The Book of Divine Works*, which lists and describes three hundred plants, some flying animals (birds, bats, insects), mammals, the elements (earth, air, water, rivers), precious stones (like emeralds, crystals, rubellites), and metals (iron, lead, silver, tin, and so on). She also wrote *Causes and Cures of Hildegard of Bingen*, wherein she attempted to systematize the knowledge of the time by producing a merging of the ancient world's medical theories and popular German traditions. Simultaneously, Hildegard corresponded with the princes and intellectuals of her time: Eleanor of Aquitaine, Bernard of Clairvaux, and Emperor Barbarossa. She also composed liturgical chants and hymns.

Hildegard's Cosmic Vision — an illumination of Scivias.

A Medieval Woman on the Move

Around the year 800, a leading cultural and social revolution occurred. Charlemagne had entrusted the administration of his empire and transmission of knowledge to the clergy. For greater efficiency, everything was inventoried and codified. For instance, the *Capitulare de Villis* outlined the obligations of the governors of the emperor's estates. This document covered a wide range of areas, including guilds of craftsmen, the textile trade, hunting, education, the establishment of schools, agriculture, food production, medicine, and botany. Monasteries served as the central elements of this system, blending ancient scientific knowledge (medicine, physics, mathematics, architecture, etc.) with contemporary practices. In the centuries following Charlemagne, exchanges increased between Venice and Byzantium, as well as between Northern and Southern Europe. Spices and other precious substances spread among the nobility, the bourgeoisie, and even within monasteries.

Calendar of Seasonal Activities — Anonymous Illumination.

A second revolution occurred at the end of the eleventh century. Jerusalem was no longer in Christian hands. The Seljuk troops were menacing Constantinople, seat of the Byzantine Empire. Other disruptions transformed society. In less than three centuries, Europe's population boomed from thirty-five million to more than eighty million. Hildegard taught at a key moment in history, the very center of the High Middle Ages. It was marked by relative peace and a rapid increase in the population. Significant economic, political, and cultural changes led to social reorganization and collective reflection on education and solidarity. As men left for crusades or wars, women assumed responsibilities, managed estates, and gained access to better education and greater respect. It was this precise historical context that allowed Hildegard to create with such freedom.

🌿 A Popular Encyclopedia

Hildegard, whether consciously or not, aimed to consolidate the knowledge of her time. This humanistic and universal approach, which likely explains the enduring popularity of Hildegard's work, was facilitated by the geographic location of the monasteries where she served. Disibodenberg and later Rupertsberg were situated in the Rhineland, at the center of a network of waterways. These locations connected as far as the Black Sea via the Danube and to the Mediterranean through the Rhine, Saône, and Rhône. The flourishing trade between Northern and Southern Europe, as well as with the Near East and Far East, provided her with access to a wealth of information.

It is not always easy to understand the writings of Hildegard, as her descriptions of plants or advice are intertwined with biblical references and theological

The Abbey of Disibodenberg (Mount Saint-Disibod), where Hildegard lived for thirty-nine years.

considerations. Nevertheless, Hildegard comforted countless sick individuals suffering from specific ailments, such as infections, as well as more complex conditions like depression. The symptomatology of mental illnesses did not exist at the time. Most disorders were identified as falling under "melancholy," a mood disorder theorized by Hippocrates. This profound sadness manifests as a lack of desire to live. The notion of a tragic fate permeated the Middle Ages and extended into the Renaissance.

A poignant testimony to this can be found three and a half centuries later in *Melencolia I*, the famous copper engraving by Albrecht Dürer. Hildegard was undoubtedly one of the first to take melancholy seriously. According to her, this mood disorder, specifically the presence of black bile, is inherent to humanity as a consequence of original sin: "At the moment Adam disobeyed the divine command, at that very instant, melancholy coagulated in his blood."

Melencolia I, a famous engraving by Albrecht Dürer (1514).

❧ Visionary Poet

The visions that plagued Hildegard throughout her life gave her the certainty that she was not mistaken, that her knowledge was confirmed by divine omniscience. For everything is connected: the mundane and the sacred, the natural and the celestial.

> I saw a vast, immense round tower formed of a single stone, shining with a brilliant whiteness. At its summit were three windows through which such great light burst forth that even the hollowed roof of the tower was visible, cloudless, in that light. These windows were framed with magnificent emeralds. And this tower was situated at the center of the woman's back, much like a tower placed within the walls of a city, such that this image, because of its strength, could not fall into ruin. And I saw children entering the belly of the image, radiant with great clarity.
>
> Some were endowed with golden rays from their foreheads to their feet; others with a light of a different hue. Similarly, some of them beheld a pure and lucid brilliance, while others saw a reddish and murky glow oriented toward the east. And my eyes remained open.... It is while fully awake, both day and night, that I see these things.... a light that has no origin and is so much brighter than the light surrounding the sun.[1]

Completed in 1152 and written in Latin, these visions were copied, disseminated in monasteries, and later translated into German. This work is significant not only because of its impact on the society of its time but also due to its length—more than six hundred pages! Of the ten manuscript copies of the original edition, the most beautiful

---

1   Beginning of the Fourth Vision.

one disappeared during World War II. Among these manuscripts are thirty-five remarkable miniatures, undoubtedly created under Hildegard's own direction.

✇ *Scivias*: Theological and Philosophical Principles

A collection of theological and philosophical principles, *Scivias* was Hildegard's most famous work during her lifetime. Through a cosmic vision, she outlines her conception of the universe and humanity, two creations that share a common origin. While distinct, they are intimately connected and constructed in the same proportions. Everything is reflected in everything else: humanity is a microcosm within the macrocosm of the universe. Her message, strikingly modern for its time, remains relevant today, as she asserts that while divine harmony is indisputable, it is humanity's responsibility to restore the world order it has disrupted.

Hildegard is also known for inventing an artificial or constructed language, the *Lingua Ignota*, which she wrote and spoke herself. It seems that this language and its script allowed her to quickly record ideas or images that came to mind, in a fashion akin to modern shorthand.

✇ Hildegard's Medicine

Hildegard of Bingen utilized everything nature offered for treating illnesses: plants, minerals, and animals. She compiled her medical corpus using the knowledge of her time. Scholastic and monastic medicine was primarily based on the writings of Constantine the African and, through him, on ancient physicians such as Hippocrates, Galen, and Dioscorides. Unsurprisingly, plants formed the majority of remedies. Hildegard also incorporated recipes from popular traditions, creating a quasi-scientific method through observation, classification, description, deduction, and conclusion.

She refined the theory of humors, developed in the fifth century B.C. by Hippocrates, which posited that the body is composed of four elements: water, fire, air, and earth. These four humors, characterized by four states (hot or cold, dry or wet), circulate in the body like blood. Antagonistic yet coexisting, they maintain health when balanced, and any imbalance threatens it. For Hildegard, these humors correspond to God's creation of humanity from water and earth. Therefore, the humors are not merely organic fluids, but also the material of physical and spiritual reactions.

Hildegard also adopted Aristotle's idea that the heart is the seat of the soul, asserting that one can see a person's soul "in their eyes."

The Book of Divine Works

In *The Book of Divine Works*, Hildegard describes each plant, mineral, or other object of study individually, situating them within the system of humors. For instance, horseradish and peach trees are classified as "hot," while marigold and coltsfoot are "cold and wet." The logic of this classification, not immediately apparent, is tied to Hildegard's experience, oral tradition, and the place of the studied object in nature. For example, the water lily, which lives on the water's surface, is "cold," while thyme, an aromatic herb needing sunlight and good drainage, is "hot." Roots like carrots or parsnips are mostly "cold and wet." Spices and essential-oil-bearing plants, such as borage, myrrh, or fennel, are "hot." Mediterranean plants and fruits, including olive, cedar, fig, and date trees, are also "hot." This approach is not entirely systematic, as additional criteria are considered for organizing simples, vegetables, and fruits.

Nature as a Treasure Hunt

The theory of signatures, developed by Aristotle and later systematized by Paracelsus four centuries later, associates elements—typically plants—with parts of the human body. For instance, clover, cherries, blackberry juice, and wine are red, and therefore deemed beneficial for the blood.

Another example is lungwort, whose leaves resemble lungs and feature lines akin to the alveoli of the bronchi; accordingly, lungwort is used to treat lung ailments, as its name suggests. Hildegard adopts the foundational principles of this theory, enriching it with the humoral system. For instance, the lungs are often affected by cold or moist humors because they expel mucus. Lungwort, being dry, helps heal the lungs. However, as a plant that grows in shaded woodlands, it is also cold. To balance the remedy and treat the lungs effectively, lungwort must be warmed.

Hildegard's *Book of Causes and Remedies* collects her reflections on dysfunctions that lead to humoral imbalances and the onset of illnesses. More theoretical than *The Book of Divine Works*, it covers a wide range of topics. The first chapter addresses cosmology (stars, elements, winds), the second examines human nature (humoral balance, sexuality, sleep, the menstrual cycle), the third explores ailments (madness, dysentery, pain), and the fourth discusses remedies. Throughout, Hildegard emphasizes the inscrutable will of God and the necessity of living a healthy and pious life. Regarding gout, she writes: "Under the influence of excessive drinking, [gout] strikes a limb suddenly.... These humors destroy the limbs they attack unless checked by divine grace and the spirit of life that animates every human."

❧ The Importance of a Balanced Diet

Hildegard believed that disease prevention hinged on proper nutrition. She recommended fasting for several hours between meals and taking a digestive walk. In *Causes and Remedies*, she writes that while a weak or sick person may need to eat in the morning, "it is healthy and necessary for a person to abstain from food until at least midday to ensure proper digestion." The issue of snacking between meals was already recognized in the Middle Ages! In the evening, she advised waiting a few hours before eating and taking a short walk before sleeping.

Fruits and vegetables, which contain "juices and moisture," should be eaten during a hot meal and with bread, as she explains: "Once you have consumed some food, you can eat these items, which will bring more health than illness." Among fruits and vegetables, Hildegard especially recommended apples, chestnuts, almonds, quinces, beans, dandelions, horseradish, and fennel, to be eaten with grains like spelt. She also noted the effectiveness of specific foods for certain ailments and provided recipes for these in the final part of this work.

❧ Wine, Beer, or Water

In the Middle Ages, beverage options were limited, since milk and fruit juices did not keep well. This left water, wine, or beer. Hildegard, rightly cautious, distrusted water that was not directly sourced. She warned: "Any other waters, if consumed without being boiled, are harmful," whether rainwater or river water. She advised diluting wine if it was too strong. Wine was also a component in numerous remedies.

As for beer, Hildegard lived at the time when hops were first introduced into its brewing process. This innovation became a defining feature of beer recipes. Monks, primarily in Alsace, Bavaria, and the Rhineland, perfected the fermentation and brewing processes for beer. This innovation provided a cheap, low-alcohol alternative to water, which was often unsafe to drink.

🌿 Science Confirms Hildegard Was Right

To modern readers, some of Hildegard's medical principles might seem simplistic. However, in her time, nature was mysterious, and understanding it required relying on tradition, alchemical research, or the study of ancient texts. The "signature" of a plant, confirmed through practice, was the primary method of experimentation. Much later, with the invention of the microscope and advances in chemistry, researchers frequently validated the empirical indications attributed to various plant, animal, and mineral substances.

Monks Brewing Beer, *an engraving by Jost Amman (1568).*

Skeptics might dismiss these findings as coincidental, yet many phytotherapeutic properties described by Hildegard have been scientifically confirmed. For instance, calendula, widely used in dermatological creams today, is the same marigold that Hildegard recommended as a poultice for scalp and skin conditions.

❧ A Skilled Musician

Hildegard's extraordinary life was shaped by monastic activities, which included medical care, cultivating medicinal herbs, prayer, and liturgical singing. During her lifetime, composing music was a contentious issue within the Church, especially if the composer was a woman. Aliette de Laleu, a music critic and journalist, noted in an interview with Radio France:

> Not all convents and monasteries embraced music. Some praised God through music, while others preferred silence to aid prayer. Hildegard of Bingen was unequivocal: she claimed that music was a way to heal the human soul.

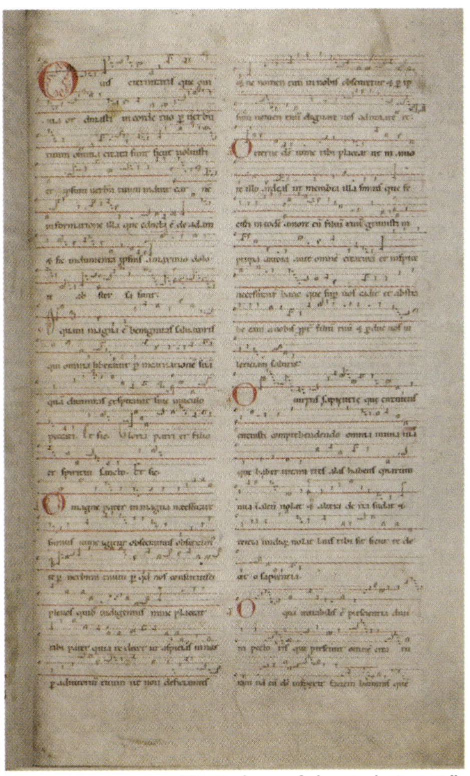

"Antiphon of the Holy Spirit" by Hildegard of Bingen.

Hildegard composed remarkably original music, exploring diverse styles, including monophonic chant, dissonances, and ornamentations. More than seventy liturgical poems—masterpieces of medieval music—have survived.

One example, a hymn to the Virgin Mary, exemplifies her spiritual and poetic vision:

> O most noble of plants, rooted in the sun,
> And in serene innocence, shining as you turn,
> No earthly fame can grasp your splendor,
> You are encircled by divine mysteries.
> You blush like the dawn and burn like a flame.

Hildegard also wrote *Ordo Virtutum*, a liturgical drama that was highly innovative for its time. She silenced critics with a radiant proclamation: "God must be praised with all the instruments invented by wise and ingenious humans."

Hildegard's Legacy

Hildegard died on September 17, 1179, at the age of 81. According to legend, on the day of her death, two rainbows formed a luminous, colorful cross above her convent. Hildegard of Bingen was an unquestionable leading figure during her lifetime with her visions, healing, and music. She was admired by the pope, St. Bernard of Clairvaux, and the emperor. Upon her death, she was buried at the Rupertsberg monastery, which was tragically destroyed and burned during the Thirty Years' War in 1632. Her relics were rescued by Benedictine nuns and preserved in the chapel of the Eibingen priory until 1929. On the 750th anniversary of her death, the relics were transferred to the church of Rüdesheim am Rhein and placed in a new shrine. Each year, on September 17, processions with her relics take place. In 1965, German pilgrims brought a coffer containing some of Hildegard's and St. Bernard of Clairvaux's relics to the Lourdes sanctuary, where they are now housed in the Pax Christi chapel.

Despite her widespread veneration, Hildegard was not officially canonized by the Catholic Church. Worse still, the Middle Ages fell into disrepute, and Hildegard's works were largely forgotten. The advent of modern medicine and chemical pharmaceuticals further discredited traditional and natural remedies.

From Purgatory to the Pantheon

Labeled as a sort of German Nostradamus and dismissed as a pseudo-saint due to her imperfect Latin, Hildegard's reputation languished in obscurity. Even her visions were questioned, with psychoanalysts and psychiatrists attributing them to symptoms of deprivation. Yet the sublime beauty of her music, the power of her visions, and the precision of her botanical monographs eventually rescued her from this semi-forgotten state, elevating her to the pantheon of Church fathers and mothers.

In the 1960s and 1970s, the hippie movement's embrace of nature, psychedelic rock, and medieval and Eastern inspirations helped to revive interest in Hildegard. Sensibility and the mysterious were placed on par with science and Cartesian rationalism, and in this cultural milieu, Hildegard was rediscovered.

In France, her resurgence gained momentum in 1994 with Régine Pernoud's biography *Hildegard of Bingen*. In 1996, Jérôme Millon publishers released Pierre Monat's translations of *The Book of Divine Works* and *Causes and Remedies*, which remain definitive. From 1997, Laurence Moulinier, a medievalist, published in-depth articles on Hildegard in academic journals. Around the same time, my own research began, focusing on the extraordinary creativity of this exceptional figure.

In Germany, the movement to rehabilitate Hildegard gained even greater traction, with extensive searches for manuscripts beginning in the 1970s. Catholic faithful began to question why Hildegard, often informally called St. Hildegard, had never been canonized. This oversight was rectified in 2012 when Pope Benedict XVI proclaimed her a Doctor of the Church, placing her on par with luminaries such as Catherine of Siena and Teresa of Ávila.

❧ A Timeless Legacy

Today, Hildegard's musical, literary, and medical works endure as a testament to her genius. She herself described the diamond as a metaphor for her legacy:

> Like a crystalline glass, it appears within viscous masses as if it were their all-powerful core. And because it is solid and hard, it bursts through the surrounding mountain mass even before it grows.

Hildegard's work is a luminous, unbreakable diamond, offering insights we have yet to fully uncover. Through her fascinating cosmogony and her understanding of the interconnectedness between causes and remedies, Hildegard challenges us to explore the boundaries of reality. Her legacy invites reflection on the human condition and the origins of the earth. Thanks to her, we are reminded to focus on what is essential and to seek the diamond—her diamond and our own—"within the viscous masses."

Part 2

Hildegard's Garden

Agrimony

Agrimonia eupatoria

This tall herb with clusters of yellow flowers sways elegantly up to 1 meter high. Generally, as yellow-flowered plants are not rare, *Agrimonia eupatoria* can be recognized by its reddish, hairy stem, which has at its base a rosette of leaves interspersed with smaller leaflets. Perennial and rhizomatous, it is common throughout Europe. The seeds have hooked hairs, facilitating their dispersal by animals. The leaves, with a lemony flavor, can be eaten raw in salads or cooked with other vegetables. The stem was historically used as the raw material for producing a yellow dye.

Though not a major medicinal plant—unlike garlic, mint, or nettle—agrimony possesses numerous properties that did not escape Hildegard of Bingen's notice. The plant is anti-inflammatory, astringent, antidepressant, cholagogue (stimulating the liver), antipruritic (soothing itching), hemostatic (stopping bleeding), and decongestant.

Hildegard provides four recipes involving agrimony. Three of them are quite complex to prepare. One recipe for pills to "rid the patient of excess saliva, secretions, and discharges" combines hyssop, benzoin, fennel, and geranium, among other ingredients. More simply, Hildegard advises washing the head of those "who have lost wisdom and good sense" with an agrimony decoction and applying a warm poultice of the plant to their abdomen: "thus, their madness will disappear." Indeed, it has been scientifically proven that *Agrimonia eupatoria* has genuine calming, anti-inflammatory, and antidepressant properties due to its richness in active compounds.

As an infusion, the flowers are recommended for combating psychological disorders. The roots, in decoctions, are used to prepare lotions for nervous agitation or ointments to alleviate skin problems. Agrimony is also applied externally to minor wounds, used in mouthwashes or eye drops. Massaging the legs with an agrimony decoction improves circulation and helps prevent varicose veins.

Agrimonia Eupatoria

Published by W. Phillips Dec.ʳ 1ˢᵗ 1805.

Garlic

Allium sativum

This advice from Hildegard is all the more relevant since some people are intolerant to garlic, and in large quantities, it can cause nausea. The garlic bulb is a root bulb composed of multiple cloves. Garlic flowers are also edible.

The primary active compound in garlic is allicin, a sulfur compound with bactericidal, antiseptic, and diuretic properties. Other components, including trace elements (iodine, silica, selenium), polyphenols, and vitamins, make garlic a medicinal food that promotes circulation, cleanses the urinary system, and helps prevent hypertension and respiratory infections. Garlic is also believed to have anti-cancer properties. Unfortunately, it can be hard on sensitive stomachs and causes strong breath. To mitigate this issue, chewing a few anise or cumin seeds suffices.

In cooking, garlic pairs with nearly all dishes except desserts. It enhances salads, meats, and fish. It's best not to expose it to heat for too long: opt for a quick, high flame, as prolonged cooking destroys some of its delicate compounds. Add garlic toward the end of sauce preparation. When used raw, mince it finely or crush it to release beneficial substances that will permeate the rest of your dish. Garlic is not recommended for breastfeeding women as it can alter milk and cause colic in infants.

In the garden, garlic, with its large white or blue flowers, is highly decorative. There are three main categories of garlic. Autumn garlic is harvested from April to July. Spring garlic is planted by March and harvested in July. Finally, stick garlic, the only variety that produces true flowering stems, is harvested starting in mid-June. Plant garlic away from asparagus, peas, and beans. When buried at the base of fruit trees, garlic bulbs repel fungal diseases and improve harvest yields.

Allium sativum L. **Knoblauch.**

Aloe

Aloe vera

Although it thrives in dry, warm soils, the remarkable aloe vera is not part of the cactus family but belongs to the order *Liliales*, like colchicum or lilies! It has evergreen leaves and shallow roots. It is easily propagated by detaching the offshoots (aerial shoots) from its roots. Cultivated since antiquity, aloe vera is found in many tropical, subtropical, and Mediterranean regions.

Aloe vera is composed of up to 99% water, but its true value lies in its active components — nearly a hundred in total — including minerals, vitamins, and amino acids, making it a renowned remedy. The plant has been a part of traditional pharmacopoeia in the Middle East and North Africa. To reach remote parts of Northern Europe and withstand long journeys by mule or ship, it was preserved in oil or alcohol — or dried and ground into powder.

Hildegard of Bingen held aloe vera in such high regard that she mentioned it twice in *The Book of Divine Works*. She recommended it in poultices for abdominal pain and, for respiratory issues, on the chest. The recipe for this poultice is simple: mash aloe vera pulp and mix it with olive oil. The resulting paste can be gently warmed in a pan before being wrapped in a clean cloth. For liver problems, she suggested a cold maceration: "For jaundice, let aloe soak in cold water and drink it morning and night before bed."

It is true that aloe vera possesses anti-inflammatory, antibiotic, and healing properties. For external use, the fresh plant is prepared by scraping out the mucilaginous central pulp from the leaf. This viscous, transparent, and bitter pulp degrades quickly due to oxidation when exposed to air, limiting its use to those with fresh leaves on hand. Poultices and massages with aloe are recommended for eczema, minor wounds, irritations, fungal infections, or rheumatism.

Aloe vera is also edible, but excessive ingestion can cause miscarriage or intestinal disorders.

Redouté pinx.

ALOE vulgaris. ALOÈS vulgaire.

Almond

Prunus amygdalus or *Amygdalus communis*

In Hildegard's time, the almond tree was highly esteemed not only for its culinary and therapeutic qualities but also as a symbol of love and virginity. This is because it is one of the few fruit trees whose flowers bloom in winter, well before the leaves. Each branch is adorned with white or pinkish petals, resembling a bridal gown.

The almond is a nut encased in a small peach-like fruit with a velvety skin. Inside, there is a second shell, yellow and woody. Only by breaking this shell can one access one or two seeds, called "almonds." The almond itself is protected by a brown skin. The sweet almond (*Prunus dulcis*), the one we eat, is the result of horticultural selection. Wild almonds, or bitter almonds, are toxic due to their high cyanide content. Almonds are very rich in unsaturated fatty acids, proteins, carbohydrates, and vitamins. Eating a few fresh almonds before meals can help reduce heartburn.

Almonds are widely used in perfumery, confectionery, and baking, especially in North Africa and Provence. For example, the *calisson* from Aix-en-Provence and the *briouate* from Agadir or Marrakesh are mainly made of almonds and sugar. Almonds are also found in energy bars and as a drink (almond milk) for those who are lactose intolerant. Almond essential oil is used in cosmetics and dermatology, relieving eczema and reportedly lightening freckles.

The almond tree needs light, sunshine, and dry air. While the tree itself can withstand frost, its flowers cannot. It thrives in Mediterranean regions. Plant it in autumn and water it well at the base during droughts. Almonds are harvested in September and October.

Amygdalus communis L.
var. amara D.C.

Dill

Anethum graveolens

Highly aromatic, dill is digestive, appetizing, antispasmodic, and diuretic. Hildegard also recommends the plant for nosebleeds and for men wishing to "extinguish the passions and pleasures of the flesh." One might doubt that this is a priority for contemporary individuals, but if it were, they would need to mix equal parts of dill, caper spurge (*Euphorbia lathyris*), and iris, then add two parts water balm (*Mentha aquatica*), and combine everything in vinegar. This resulting condiment should season all their meals.

Dill's reputation in the Middle Ages was such that it was routinely given to guests who overindulged at banquets. It was included among the crops Charlemagne recommended for his royal estates.

Today, dill is a universal condiment for a variety of dishes. Its fresh or dried leaves add flavor to salads, fish, cheese, meats, sauces, and soups. The flowers and seeds are used to flavor wines, preserves, and jams.

A true aromatic herb, like cumin, mint, thyme, or rosemary, dill is not merely a digestive aid. It promotes lactation in young mothers, soothes epileptic seizures (one of the few known remedies for this until the nineteenth century), and encourages sleep. Dill is an ingredient in many medicinal wines, such as one proposed by Hildegard, but its leaves and flowers are most commonly consumed as a tea.

Growing 80 to 150 cm tall, dill has finely divided leaves. Its flowers spread in lovely yellow-green umbels. In French, dill is also called "bastard fennel" or "false anise." While related to these plants, its umbels may cause confusion, though its scent does not. To always have fresh leaves available, sow regularly starting in April. Dill thrives in sunny exposures and well-drained soil.

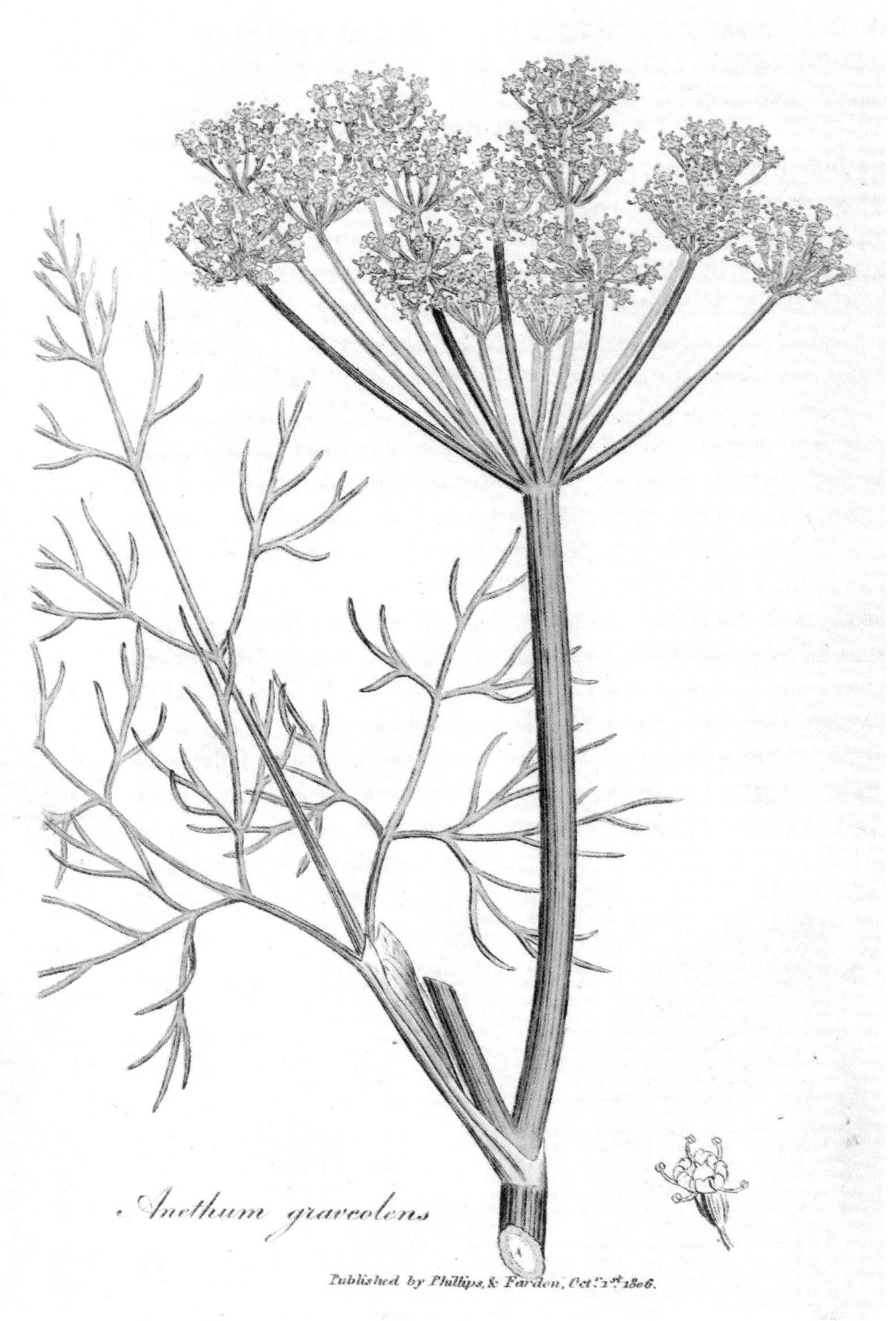

Anethum graveolens

Published by Phillips, & Fardon, Oct.r 2.d 1806.

Angelica

Angelica archangelica

Angelica, also known as the "herb of the angels," owes its name to its therapeutic properties, its majestic stature, and its characteristic suave, musky fragrance. It is one of the ingredients in Hildegard's theriac.

This stunning herbaceous plant grows over two meters tall. Its flowers form an impressive pale green or white umbel. *Angelica sylvestris*, the wild variety, is found in woods and clearings across Europe. To distinguish it from the dangerous hemlock, simply crush a few leaves: angelica emits a pleasant aroma, while hemlock has a repulsive stench reminiscent of cat urine, making confusion unlikely.

The cultivated *Angelica archangelica* was grown in medicinal gardens, such as those of Hildegard's abbey. In monasteries, it was believed to treat plague and rabies. Although no antibiotic could effectively combat these devastating zoonoses, angelica, with its recognized bactericidal properties, could occasionally provide relief to sufferers. Beyond its antibacterial action, angelica is known for its aperitif qualities and is antiviral, anti-inflammatory, gastro-protective, anticonvulsive, sedative, diuretic, and vasodilatory. Its root is an excellent tonic.

The infusion is delightful, slightly peppery with a hint of licorice. Decoctions are used in compresses or lotions for massages to relieve muscular and joint pain. Combined with nettle, it strengthens hair. Angelica essential oil has sedative, digestive, and anticoagulant properties, making it suitable for anxiety, nervous fatigue, insomnia, and sleep disorders. Its flowers, seeds, and stems are used in baking, confectionery, and liqueurs. Tender leaves can serve as a condiment to flavor salads and soups.

In the garden, angelica is sown from July to September, preferably near nettles, which enhance its essential oil production. Harvest occurs in the third year for seeds, which must be sown quickly.

Adverse effects

This plant should be avoided during pregnancy, as it may pose risks. Additionally, it is known to increase sensitivity to sunlight; therefore, consuming it before sun exposure is ill-advised. Avoid applying its sap directly to the skin, as it can cause irritation. Handle with care and respect for its potency.

31

Oats

Avena sativa

There are primarily two types of oats: cultivated oats (*Avena sativa*) and wild oats (*Avena fatua*). The latter is considered a weed, with fibrous roots that are difficult to eradicate due to their deep penetration into the soil. Oats are grown both as a cereal for human consumption and as forage for animals. Horses, in particular, delight in its tender, sweet stems. More than a hundred varieties (cultivars) of *Avena sativa* exist. For poultices or teas, *Avena fatua* can also be used, though its specific application in phytotherapy is relatively recent and originates from Indian Ayurvedic medicine.

While Hildegard praises oats' nourishing properties, she does so without particular enthusiasm, recommending them only for those in good health. Nonetheless, numerous studies have demonstrated the benefits of oats in regulating cholesterol and blood sugar levels. According to the World Health Organization, oat proteins are comparable in quality to those found in meat, milk, or eggs. Researchers have also confirmed oats' calming effects on the nervous system and their soothing properties for the skin.

Oats are commonly consumed in the form of oatmeal, porridge, biscuits, or mixed with other flours. With the resurgence of interest in natural therapies and healthy eating, oat milk has become readily available in health food sections as a replacement for animal milk.

Oatmeal Tip

To relieve skin problems and rheumatism, apply a poultice of flakes or grains directly to the skin; secure it with a cloth.

Oat Allergies

The oat protein, avenin, can cause a reaction less commonly recognized, but sometimes just as debilitating, as gluten intolerance.

Avena sativa.

Burdock

Arctium lappa

For Hildegard and ancient physicians, burdock was recommended to eliminate kidney stones, address respiratory problems, and, most notably, treat or prevent skin conditions. Roman actors placed burdock leaves under their masks to minimize the irritating effects of leather on their sweaty skin.

Taller than a man, burdock grows along embankments or in debris-filled areas, thriving in poorly drained, nitrogen-rich soil. Its large leaves, with a downy underside, distinguish it from similar varieties. The flowers are small balls with beautiful purple petals, surrounded by spiny bracts. The fleshy, long root is brown on the outside and white inside. Its fruits are brown achenes that cling to animal fur for dispersal. Children often playfully toss them onto each other's hair or clothes.

Burdock is rich in B vitamins and minerals, including calcium, iron, potassium, sodium, magnesium, and phosphorus. Most importantly, it contains an antibacterial and virucidal essential oil. It is a purifying, antimicrobial plant with tonic properties, regulating the liver and the circulatory system. Recent scientific research has also revealed that burdock possesses aphrodisiac, hormone-stimulating, hypoglycemic, and tissue-regenerating properties.

Wrapped in a clean cloth and stored in a cellar or the lower part of a refrigerator, the roots can be kept for several days—long enough for a thorough detox regimen. Burdock root decoctions can be consumed, used as a gargle for dental issues, or applied as a lotion for skin or hair care.

In the garden, although burdock requires nitrogen, it is not overly demanding. Regular compost applications are sufficient. Propagation is done by direct seeding in June or July, allowing for a harvest until mid-November. However, waiting more than five months risks harvesting overly fibrous roots.

Arctium Lappa.

Published by Phillips & Farden, March.1.ᵗ 1805.

Basil

Ocimum basilicum

The symptoms Hildegard describes resemble stammering, stage fright, or shyness, which is unsurprising since basil, in addition to its renowned digestive properties, has calming and anti-anxiety effects. It is recommended for intellectual overwork, anxiety, migraines, and insomnia. Basil has also been shown to be beneficial for numerous other conditions, including nausea, respiratory issues, and intestinal disorders.

Rich in phytohormones, basil enhances and regulates insufficient menstrual flow. In weight-loss diets, it curbs cravings. Globally considered an aphrodisiac, basil is a key ingredient in love potions. The plant carries a dual symbolism—both funerary and erotic. Folklore suggests women in love should rub basil flowers on their lower abdomen to enhance their allure.

Basil has square stems and oval green leaves, blooming from June to September. To encourage the growth of new leaves, it is best to trim the flowering tops. Basil leaves are preferably eaten raw, as cooking diminishes both their properties and aroma. They are the essential ingredient in Provençal *pistou* and Italian pesto, often served with pasta. Whether raw or cooked, basil leaves aid digestion in a variety of dishes, including soups, fish, meats, salads, and cheeses. Basil also promotes lactation in nursing mothers.

It is also used in infusions, as a rub, or in the form of essential oil, which is strongly antiseptic and supports respiratory health. Two main varieties are commonly cultivated: small-leaf basil and common basil, whose leaves grow up to 5 cm in length. Basil requires good sunlight exposure and well-drained soil. It is sown from April to October, and the seeds should not be covered, as they need light to germinate.

Ocymum basilicum.

Boxwood

Buxus sempervireus

Boxwood is a magnificent shrub with dense, evergreen foliage that can grow up to 5 or 6 meters tall. In autumn, bees are drawn to its fruit for the sweet nectar. The glossy, dark green leaves, lighter on the underside, release a peculiar odor reminiscent of cat urine when crushed.

The art of topiary, or boxwood sculpture, originated in ancient Rome and flourished in the cloisters of medieval monasteries and abbeys. Hildegard recommended boxwood for use in skin or eye lotions: *"Dip a feather into it and gently apply it around blemishes."*

In Hildegard's time and even today, boxwood is a staple of medicinal gardens, often used to delineate four quadrants in honor of the four evangelist apostles. These divisions allocate space for different plant varieties and help minimize cross-pollination.

Rich in alkaloids, boxwood is only sold in pharmacies under medical supervision. Infusions of boxwood leaves are potent sudorifics, challenging-to-dose laxatives, and effective anti-rheumatics. However, given its toxicity, extreme caution is advised to avoid side effects such as vomiting, diarrhea, convulsions, and respiratory issues. Composite teas containing boxwood (combined with thyme, hyssop, mullein, or borage) are permitted.

For external use, decoctions or macerations are used in lotions to invigorate the scalp, purify the skin, and relieve muscle pain. Before applying to the scalp or other areas, test the mixture on the back of the hand. To be cautious, dilution is recommended.

In the garden, boxwood is relatively easy to cultivate, though it is susceptible to diseases caused by fungi and pests like the box tree moth (*Cydalima perspectalis*).

Precaution

Women who are pregnant or breastfeeding, as well as children, should not ingest boxwood.

335. *Buxus sempervirens* L.   Immergrüner Buchsbaum.

German Chamomile

Chrysanthemum parthenium

The leaves of German chamomile are flat and broadly lobed, while those of Roman chamomile (*Chamaemelum nobile*) are small and elongated. The white flowers have a distinctive fragrance. Considered magical, chamomile is cultivated near homes to protect them. Highly esteemed throughout Northern Europe, it was among the plants mandated in Charlemagne's gardens.

Chamomile is stimulating, tonic, digestive, antispasmodic, antiseptic, vermifuge, insecticidal, and fever-reducing. As a tea, either alone or in blends, it alleviates insomnia, indigestion, flatulence, aerophagia, painful menstruation, and eczema. For chronic migraines, some people chew the flower buds or rub their temples with them. Its use is not recommended during the last months of pregnancy.

In cosmetics, chamomile extracts, in varying concentrations, are found in skin lotions, soaps, and shampoos designed to lighten hair.

Its essential oil, which is powerful (and somewhat harsh), expensive, and blue in color, should be used with caution. For neuralgia and headaches, dilute it in olive oil and massage the affected areas. When mixed in equal parts with oregano and savory essential oils, German chamomile oil is said to aid in eliminating Borrelia, the bacteria responsible for Lyme disease (2 drops of the mixture, twice a day).

In France, chamomile is commonly found growing wild. It is often cultivated near vineyards, where it protects the vines by stimulating potassium production. In gardens, chamomile should be sown directly in the soil during spring, after the last frost. To combat aphids and other pests on roses and laurels, spray them with chamomile manure—a concentrated plant maceration.

Matricaria Parthenium

Published by Phillips, & Fardon, June 1st 1806.

Cinnamon

Cinnamomum

There is no doubt that Hildegard appreciated cinnamon! She recommended it in wine, on a slice of bread, or directly in the hand to lick. According to her, the spice helps alleviate all types of fevers and respiratory issues. Indeed, cinnamon, rich in cinnamaldehyde, boasts exceptional antibacterial, antiviral, and anti-inflammatory properties.

The word "cinnamon" appeared in Hildegard's time and derives from the Latin *canna*, meaning "reed," referencing the tubular shape of cinnamon sticks. It is also consumed ground. Known since antiquity, cinnamon comes from the inner bark of the cinnamon tree. Highly aromatic, it has a warm, woody flavor. Cinnamon is rich in minerals (manganese, copper, iron, etc.), low in calories, and both appetizing and digestive. Some of its compounds, besides cinnamaldehyde, mimic insulin and help lower blood glucose levels, making it beneficial for those with type 2 diabetes.

In Europe and North America, cinnamon is commonly added to desserts, while in North Africa and the Middle East, it is used in cooking meats and poultry. Cinnamon sticks can endure long cooking times, but powdered cinnamon should only be added just before serving, as prolonged cooking makes it bitter. Before routinely adding it to desserts—it is almost impossible to find an apple pie without cinnamon in Anglo-Saxon countries—ensure your guests are not allergic or intolerant to it. Both sticks and powder should be stored in an airtight container in a cool, dry, and dark place.

Did you know?

The best cinnamon comes from Ceylon (Sri Lanka). Ceylon cinnamon has an ochre color and is composed of thin, brittle layers of bark. Chinese cinnamon, on the other hand, is reddish-brown with thicker sticks that are less sweet.

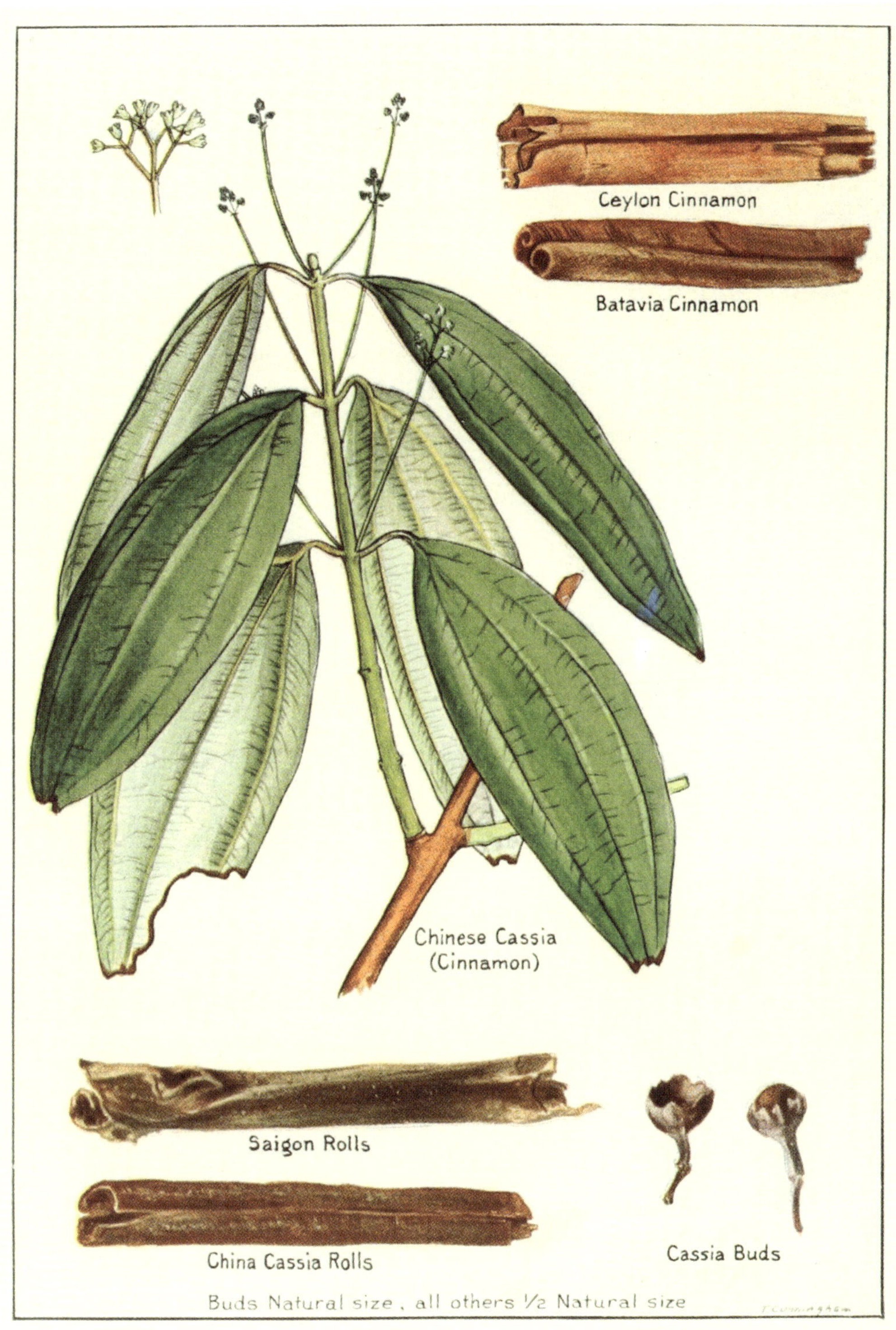

Ceylon Cinnamon
Batavia Cinnamon
Chinese Cassia
(Cinnamon)
Saigon Rolls
China Cassia Rolls
Cassia Buds
Buds Natural size , all others ½ Natural size

Carrot

Daucus carota

In Hildegard's time, carrots did not enjoy the popularity they do today. First, they were less tender, and second, they were not orange—a color that appeared much later. The root resembled a whitish, fibrous turnip. Nonetheless, carrots were among the plants recommended by Charlemagne.

Rich in vitamins and trace elements, carrots are diuretic, intestinally antiseptic, tonic, anti-anemic, mildly aphrodisiac, laxative, and anti-rheumatic, and, as Hildegard aptly stated, they "fill the human belly." This makes them an excellent vegetable for weight-loss diets, convalescence, or athletes' meals. They also contain carotene, which promotes tanning.

Carrot roots may be elongated or rounded, and their colors include orange, yellow, white, or even purple. In cooking, carrots can be enjoyed raw or cooked. They pair well with raw vegetables, meats, and other vegetables such as chard, turnips, or cardoons. They are often included in vegetable medleys or soups. Carrot greens can be used in soups or salads, and carrot juice is not only refreshing but also rich in minerals.

In gardening, it is best to avoid recently developed "F1" hybrids and instead opt for heritage or rustic varieties. The *Blanche de Kuttingen* or *Jaune du Doubs* most closely resemble the carrots cultivated in medieval monastic gardens. However, varieties like *Nantaise* or *Narbonnaise* are sweeter and more flavorful. Carrots are sown directly in the ground from February to June, without transplanting, and harvested three to five months later, depending on cultivation methods and varieties.

Carrot Poultice

Grated carrot or fresh leaf poultices relieve burns, abscesses, recent wounds, leg ulcers, or boils. Apply the crushed root or leaves. Secure with a clean bandage. Leave for two hours. Repeat the process two or three times a day.

1174

Celery

Apium graveolens

Hildegard did not recommend celery in its raw form. Until the nineteenth century, celery was rarely consumed as a vegetable. Over time, with the evolution of varieties and tastes, celery became a staple in markets.

Celery was known in antiquity for its supposed aphrodisiac properties — likely an exaggeration. Nonetheless, its richness in vitamins A, B, and C, as well as trace elements, makes it a fortifying and revitalizing food, recommended for convalescents and athletes. The properties of stalk celery (*Apium graveolens var. dulce*) and celeriac (*Apium graveolens var. rapaceum*) are comparable: both are antiseptic, diuretic, anti-rheumatic, purifying, and stomachic. Celery is also reputed to treat urinary infections. As an excellent vasodilator, it stimulates blood circulation to the brain, potentially slowing age-related cognitive decline. Low in calories and high in fiber, celery is recommended for weight-loss diets — except for those with hypertension due to its high sodium content.

Celery stalks should have fresh, green leaves. The leaves can be eaten raw in salads or added to sauces, while the stalks can be sautéed or prepared as a gratin. Celeriac, available from September, should be firm and heavy. It can be wrapped in a cloth and stored in the refrigerator. Steam-cooked celeriac is often mashed with a touch of nutmeg. For celery remoulade salad, use a dressing based on soy cream and lemon for easier digestion. Celery seeds are used as a condiment, and celery salt — kitchen salt mixed with celery extracts — adds flavor to fresh vegetables, soups, marinades, salads, and cocktails, such as the Bloody Mary.

Wild celery grows in damp areas. Its cultivation is somewhat complex (detailed later in the text). Celeriac and stalk celery are related but come from different plants.

366. *Apium graveolens* L. Gemeiner Sellerie.

Chervil

Anthriscus silvestris (wild chervil)
or *Anthriscus cerefolium* (cultivated)

Known as "wood parsley," "donkey parsley," or "white hemlock," wild chervil (*Anthriscus sylvestris*), referenced by Hildegard, is an interesting medicinal plant but can be toxic. Moreover, it is easily mistaken for poisonous relatives like hemlock. Proper identification is crucial before harvesting wild chervil (details provided later in the text). All types of chervil—including "fool's chervil," which must also be avoided—feature beautiful white umbels, resembling those of wild carrot. While wild carrot emits a carrot-like aroma when its leaves are crushed, chervil has a more anise-like scent.

Chervil is a biennial or perennial plant with an elongated root. Key distinguishing features include a green, uniformly colored, hollow, and grooved stem with slightly raised nodes (hemlock stems are spotted). Its fruits are black, smooth, and shiny. Wild chervil is considered invasive and can cover embankments and roadsides with its white flowers in spring.

Unless you are a botanical expert, it is safer to avoid harvesting wild chervil. Cultivated chervil (*Anthriscus cerefolium*), available in markets and gardens, offers the same diuretic and purifying medicinal benefits when grown organically. For external use, it has soothing and decongesting properties. Rich in vitamins C, B9, minerals, trace elements, and provitamin A, chervil has diuretic, purifying, and calming effects.

Chervil is easy to cultivate, sown directly in the ground from March to September. It prefers partial shade and cool soil. Germination takes eight to ten days. To ensure a continuous harvest, sow seeds every three weeks, as chervil loses its aroma once it flowers.

Anthriscus silvestris Hoffm.

Blessed Thistles

Centaurea benedicta

Among thistles, *Centaurea benedicta* is notable for its aggressive spines. Its magnificent yellow flower is protected by a crown of thorns amid needle-like leaves. Although invasive in some regions, blessed thistle remains a major medicinal plant, now cultivated in Romania, Estonia, and Ukraine. It has been a staple in monastic pharmacopoeia, preserved in powdered form from leaves, roots, dried flowers, or seeds. Historically, it was consumed for its digestive, stomach-aiding, and fever-reducing properties and even used in attempts to treat plague and smallpox.

Physicians of old even advised adding blessed thistle seeds to flour before baking bread. Modern chemistry has revealed the plant contains antibiotic compounds. It was one of the few common remedies for battlefield wounds. Blessed thistle stimulates the circulatory, urinary, digestive, and hepato-biliary systems and has a reputation as an aphrodisiac. It is available as a dietary supplement or infusion in natural health stores.

In many countries, blessed thistle is eaten as a vegetable or condiment. Its two-year-old roots and stems are cooked like salsify. After removing the spines, the leaves can be consumed in salads.

Blessed thistle seeds can be purchased online or from garden centers. Sow in well-drained, sunny soil in spring or autumn. The plant typically flowers in its first year. Though not frost-resistant, it self-seeds easily.

Compositae.
Cnicus benedictus L.
W.M. n.d Nat.

Chestnut

Castanea sativa

Hildegard recommended chestnuts not only for rheumatism and stomach pains but also for migraines, melancholy (depression), and what we now recognize as cardiovascular diseases. Once abundant, particularly in the Rhône Valley, chestnut forests were heavily exploited for their wood, leading to significant deforestation.

Chestnuts are rich in minerals and serve as a muscular, nervous, and blood tonic. They were a staple food in parts of Europe lacking cereal crops, earning the reputation of a nourishing fruit. Highly energizing, chestnuts combat cold and fatigue, but their high caloric content should be noted by those managing weight. The leaves and bark, rich in tannins, have sedative and expectorant properties. Infusions of chestnut leaves treat whooping cough, bronchitis, coughs, diarrhea, rheumatism, hemorrhages, and back pain. Gargles made from the leaves are used for sore throats.

Chestnuts, a winter fruit or vegetable, pair well with white meats and sauces. Boil them briefly to make peeling easier. Once steamed, chestnuts can be made into purées or stuffing for fish and poultry.

Chestnut trees are rarely grown in gardens due to their size. They have thick bark that spirals around the trunk. Large, pointed leaves adorn the tree, which produces both male and female flowers. Female flowers develop in small clusters encased in a husk, which later becomes the shell protecting the chestnut. Store chestnuts in sand in a cool cellar.

53

Cabbage

Brassica oleracea

Hildegard's mistrust of cabbage stems from two reasons. First, according to Hippocratic principles, she described it as "cold and barely dry in nature," which made it unsuitable. Second, its richness in sulfur compounds makes it less digestible, particularly if not prepared carefully.

In ancient Greece, cabbage was thought to cure hangovers—a claim not entirely unfounded. Roman soldiers used cabbage leaves as poultices to heal wounds. Included among the plants Charlemagne recommended for royal domains, cabbage was more a medicinal plant than a vegetable until the late Middle Ages.

Cabbage has gastric and intestinal healing properties, stimulates the liver and kidneys, and is rich in vitamins, minerals, and glucosinolate, a healing compound. While low in calories, its sulfur content can cause allergic reactions, gastric reflux, or bloating. To avoid these issues, blanch cabbage for two to three minutes in boiling water without a lid, then discard the water. This step removes sulfur compounds and makes cabbage easier to digest in any preparation—whether sautéed, steamed, baked, or in stews.

For detox or nutrient preservation, raw cabbage is preferred. Externally, crushed leaves (four to five) can be applied to wounds, varicose veins, or eczema and secured with a bandage. Leave overnight and rinse in case of irritation.

Cabbage should not be planted near garlic, fennel, leeks, or other crucifers. Avoid planting it on the same plot for consecutive years to prevent disease and nutrient depletion.

Braſsicaoleracea capitata.
Gemeiner Kopfkohl.

Quince

Cydonia oblonga or *Cydonia communis*

Hildegard also recommended cooked quince in poultices for ulcers or fetid infections. The symbolism of cunning attributed to quince reflects medieval anthropomorphism, where the traits of plants or animals were linked to their appearance. Quince, associated with marriage, also symbolized temptation. Biblical exegetes sometimes considered quince, rather than the apple, as the forbidden fruit, tying it to the serpent and the idea of cunning.

The quince tree (*Cydonia oblonga*) is a small, bushy tree with a gnarled trunk and deciduous foliage. Its white or pink flowers bloom in May, yielding large yellow fruits. Rich in potassium, vitamin C, pectin, and fiber, quince is known for regulating intestinal transit. Decoctions of quince seeds are used to treat pneumonia internally and hemorrhoids externally.

Due to its astringency and granular texture, quince is not eaten raw. Cooked, it is transformed into jellies, compotes, cakes, candied fruit, or fruit pastes. It can be baked and stuffed with sugar like apples. After prolonged cooking, its pulp turns red. In Hispanic countries, quince is used to make the delicious *dulce de membrillo*. It is also featured in some tagine recipes.

Quince trees thrive in various soils, resist frost, and are low-maintenance but should be planted in sheltered areas to avoid cold winds. Quince fruits, covered with a light fuzz, are ready for harvest when the fuzz no longer clings to the fingers.

Cydonia vulgaris Pers.

Cumin

Cuminum cyminum

Hildegard recommends cumin only for healthy individuals. Some translators interpret "vapors" as conditions like asthma, dizziness, or hot flashes, which Hildegard considers minor or temporary ailments. In her recipes, she pairs cumin with other spices like pepper and green anise. She also suggests using it on bread: *"You can also eat powdered cumin spread on bread; it soothes the hot and cold humors in the intestines that cause nausea."*

Cumin has been cultivated for its seeds, which have been prized since antiquity. Its aromatic, peppery flavor earned it a place among the most esteemed spices. This herbaceous plant, part of the parsley family (*Apiaceae*), produces white or pink umbels of flowers, and its oval, brown seeds are used for their digestive, anti-inflammatory, and diuretic properties. Cumin stimulates lactation and relieves menstrual pain and is also known as an aphrodisiac.

In her *Book of Divine Works*, Hildegard also mentions "black cumin," referring to nigella (*Nigella sativa*), an herb with similar properties.

Cumin is a versatile spice, enhancing dishes like curry, chili, and masala. It can also be consumed as an infusion, alone or combined with plants like fennel or anise. A decoction of crushed seeds is used as a lotion or poultice.

Cuminum Cyminum L.

Spelt

Triticum spelta

Hildegard repeatedly praises spelt, recommending it for combating depression, melancholy, and regaining strength during illness or convalescence.

Cultivated in Germany since the time of the Celts, spelt is a highly rustic cereal considered the ancestor of wheat. It differs from wheat by its grain, which remains covered in its husk at harvest. Spelt is rich in fiber, aiding digestion, and is a good source of vitamins (A, B, and E) and minerals (sodium, calcium, potassium, magnesium, silicon, phosphorus, sulfur, iron, and zinc). It contains all eight essential amino acids, which help build muscle mass, and its gluten promotes satiety. Its slow-releasing sugars combat fatigue, particularly during the day or after physical activity. Spelt also reduces blood sugar and cholesterol levels, making it a remarkable dietary and nutritional grain.

The only drawback is its gluten, which some people are intolerant to. Symptoms like unexplained fatigue, abdominal pain, irregular digestion, anxiety attacks, or fungal infections may indicate gluten sensitivity. In such cases, stop consuming gluten for a few days and consult a doctor.

For the majority of people, spelt is an excellent ingredient for soups, salads, or risottos with porcini mushrooms. Soak the grains overnight before cooking them in boiling water or steaming. Hildegard advises adding fat or an egg yolk to make spelt easier to swallow. It has a nutty flavor and stays crunchy even when well-cooked. Spelt flour can be used for bread and delicious pastries.

T. 29
Triticum zea

Fennel

Foeniculum vulgare

Fennel is a tall plant with yellow umbels that can reach up to two meters in height and is easily recognized by its dill-like fragrance. As Hildegard noted, every part of the plant has medicinal uses. The bulbous base of its leaves and stem is primarily used in cooking. The roots, with diuretic properties, relieve rheumatism and urinary infections. Fennel seeds are aperitive and digestive, classified among the "four hot seeds" of antiquity (alongside green anise, coriander, and caraway) for their carminative properties, aiding in the expulsion of intestinal gas and improving digestion. Fennel also soothes nausea, bloating, and stomach aches.

However, fennel contains an essential oil rich in estrogen, making it unsuitable for pregnant women or those with uterine conditions. In moderation, it stimulates lactation in nursing mothers.

Fennel, available fresh from May, has an anise-like flavor. Choose fennel with a strong aroma and fresh, green feathery leaves. Store it in the refrigerator's vegetable drawer, away from other vegetables, to prevent flavor transfer. Fennel enhances the taste of meats and fish. All parts are edible: the bulb, the stems, and even the feathery tops for seasoning. Popular recipes include braised, roasted, gratins, raw in salads with carrots, oranges, or green apples, or made into purées, pestos, or tarts. Avoid boiling fennel in water to preserve its flavor and nutrients. For freezing, slice and blanch for a few minutes.

Fennel thrives in sunny, well-drained soil. Sow or transplant it away from crucifers but near cucurbits, mint, or sage. Harvest from August to November.

Foeniculum capillaceum Gilib.

Broad Beans, also known as Fava Beans

Vicia faba

Did you know?

In ancient Rome, during the Saturnalia celebrating the winter solstice, voting tokens to designate the king of the banquet were dried beans. This is the origin of the fève in the Galette des Rois.

This annual legume, cultivated for millennia, produces seeds rich in protein and starch, used for both human consumption and animal fodder. Its flowers feature a large white corolla with purple veins, composed of five unequal petals, with the upper petal larger than the lateral "wings."

Broad beans are primarily grown in the Mediterranean region. Fresh beans are sold in early summer and have a flavor distinct from dried ones. Rich in plant proteins, carbohydrates, vitamins B and C, and minerals, broad beans are low-calorie, high-fiber legumes, making them a dietary aid. They improve intestinal transit but should be consumed in moderation to avoid straining the colon. Their potassium, phosphorus, iron, and vitamins make them a stimulant for convalescents, the fatigued, or those experiencing intellectual overwork.

Favism, a rare hereditary intolerance to certain bean substances, can cause abnormal red blood cell destruction when amplified by certain medications.

Once shelled, beans may have their thick white skin removed if too tough. Boiled broad beans are eaten in stews, purées, or soups. Raw beans can be enjoyed with butter on bread or in salads.

Broad beans grow in most soil types but prefer well-drained soils. Harvest approximately three months after sowing.

XVII. 3. 100. Leguminosae
Vicia Faba L.
Saubohne.

Fern

Dryopteris filix

In her extensive chapter on fern, Hildegard discusses witchcraft practices, suggesting that carrying fern protects against them. Another "good magic" practice, widespread across Europe, involved young women collecting ferns on the eve of St. John's Day to win the hearts of desired men.

Hildegard also recognized the medicinal properties of ferns, which "purify the eyes," "alleviate arthritis," and treat deafness, memory disorders, and "paralysis of the tongue." She was aware of the plant's effects on the nervous system.

Ferns, unlike other plants, have a unique reproduction system, and their leaves are known as "fronds." They thrive along hedgerows, shaded slopes, and forested areas. The "male fern" (*Dryopteris filix-mas*) is more robust with broader fronds than the "female fern" (*Dryopteris filix*). Both varieties (Hildegard does not distinguish between them) have rhizomes used in decoctions as a vermifuge and for treating liver flukes in sheep. Harvestable year-round, the root is regulated and only sold in pharmacies due to its toxicity in high doses. Fronds have anti-inflammatory properties and are applied to rheumatism. Certain phytochemicals, such as triterpenes and filicin, exhibit calming and sedative effects on the central nervous system, easing pain and promoting sleep. In some regions, ferns are even placed inside pillows.

Fern bouquets were traditionally used to repel flies and ward off curses. Following Hildegard's advice, ferns can be planted around the home. They are low-maintenance but prefer shade and humidity.

XXIV.
2. Poly.
B
A
1
2
Wurmfarn.
10 A. Aspidium filix mas Swartz.
B. Aspidium lobatum Swartz.
WM

Gentian

Gentiana lutea

Vigilance!

The harvesting of yellow gentian, purple gentian (*Gentiana purpurea*), or spotted gentian (*Gentiana punctata*) is regulated in certain regions. Moreover, especially when it has lost its flowers, yellow gentian can be confused with white hellebore (*Veratrum album*), which is highly toxic. It is therefore recommended to use only roots purchased from herbalists or ready-made preparations.

Once again, Hildegard's advice proves sound. Gentian strengthens the body in general and the digestive system in particular. Known since antiquity, it was a key ingredient in theriac, a legendary elixir comprising around fifty plants and animal extracts (such as viper venom and beaver glands), reputed to cure all diseases and poisonings. The recipe for the "grand" theriac was a closely guarded secret, requiring several months of preparation. For more common ailments, the simpler "German theriac," mainly composed of gentian, aristolochia, bay berries, myrrh, juniper, and honey, was preferred. This elixir, sometimes referred to as "Hildegard's elixir," is still commercially available.

Yellow gentian (*Gentiana lutea*), also known as great or officinal gentian, is found in most European mountain ranges. Its tall yellow flowers cluster at the base of upper leaves. After about ten years, its roots are harvested during the warmer months using a specialized fork. Rich in bitter glucosides, the roots are used to produce beverages like liqueurs, beers, and aperitifs, and are also available as teas. Gentian is renowned for treating digestive issues and appetite loss. It serves as an antiseptic, stimulates the immune system, and is recommended for convalescence and chronic fatigue.

69

Ginger

Zingiber officinale

Hildegard was deeply cautious about ginger, which carried a dubious reputation as an aphrodisiac and magical plant. Its warmth could stimulate the senses during illness but was considered excessive for the healthy. She dedicated an extensive chapter to this renowned root, emphasizing its role in remedies for stomach ailments, digestive issues, impetigo, and eye disorders. In the Middle Ages, *hypocras* (a medicinal wine) was infused with ginger, cinnamon, and other spices.

A tropical perennial herb, ginger features fragrant evergreen leaves and white-and-yellow flowers with red markings. Its rhizome, whether fresh or dried, contains essential oils and chemical compounds responsible for its spicy flavor, warmth, and medicinal properties.

Ginger is known to alleviate migraines, motion sickness, and morning sickness. Chinese sailors chewed it to combat seasickness, and pregnant women used it to ease nausea. Ginger protects the gastric lining, reduces biliary and pancreatic insufficiencies, lowers LDL cholesterol and triglycerides, and provides anti-inflammatory relief for rheumatism. It is also thought to have anticancer effects.

Young rhizomes are juicy and mild, while mature ones are fibrous, drier, and more intensely flavored. Ginger is used in candied form, baking, and as a spice in numerous Asian dishes.

Ginger thrives in sunny, humid conditions. It is propagated from rhizome sections with growth buds, not seeds. Starting cultivation indoors or in a greenhouse is recommended.

Amomum Zinziber.

Published by W. Phillips, Feb.y 1.st 1810.

Hops

Humulus

Precaution

Hop cones (flowers) can cause skin allergies in harvesters and are toxic to dogs.

Hildegard was among the first to note hops' preservative properties for food and drink. She highlighted the antiseptic and preservative qualities of female hop cones, contributing to the rise of beer. Previously, beverages like *cervoise* were brewed using a mix of herbs and spices. Hops also impart beer's characteristic aroma and bitterness.

A climbing plant, hops grow in cool, humid environments with access to sunlight, often at forest edges or in clearings. They have robust roots and stems that twist around supports using sharp appendages. Hops are rich in resins, essential oils, proteins, and flavonoids.

Nicknamed the "vine of the North" or "wolf plant," hops possess sedative, digestive, aperitive, febrifuge, and calming properties. They treat irritability, insomnia, and excessive libido. Traditionally, hops were placed in pillows to promote sleep (and perhaps to temper spousal impulses). Rich in phytoestrogens, hops also regulate painful menstruation and stimulate lactation.

Hop flowers are consumed in beer or as herbal teas. Young shoots harvested in early spring are edible, raw in salads or cooked like asparagus, omelets, or risottos. The stems of hops in hop fields are supported by ropes that are attached to cables that connect wooden poles which are two to three meters high. The male plants are planted at a distance to avoid the production of grains that release undesirable odors as they oxydize.

XXII,5.
43. Cannabinaceae.
183. Humulus Lupulus L.   Hopfen.

Iris

Iris germanica

Hildegard recommends the use of iris both internally and externally. Recipes for powders, wines, porridges, or decoctions eliminate skin problems, slow dementia episodes, expel urinary stones, and even cure leprosy. Because of its blue color, symbolizing the Virgin Mary, and its shape resembling the lance that pierced Christ's heart, the iris also holds religious significance. The Virgin Mary is often depicted near iris flowers, such as in a striking painting by Jan Brueghel the Elder or Albrecht Dürer's *Madonna with the Iris*.

The flower stem of the iris bears four violet, blue, or white flowers. Its long leaves, arranged in a fan shape, remain evergreen in winter. Rhizomes (or corms) of certain iris varieties are toxic, but *Iris germanica* is not; when dried, it releases a pleasant fragrance. Since antiquity, iris rhizomes have been powdered for medicinal remedies and spices. Even today, they are used to flavor alcohol; dropping a rhizome into wine barrels enhances the wine.

The rhizome, rich in mucilage and tannins, has expectorant, diuretic, and purgative properties. Iris rhizomes are rubbed on babies' gums to ease teething pain. The powder, with its delightful violet scent, is soothing, calming, and deodorizing.

The iris requires rich, well-drained soil and at least half a day of sunlight. Flowers should be trimmed after blooming. The plant reproduces exclusively through rhizome division, which is recommended every four to six years in autumn to maintain growth.

Deutsche Schwertlilie.

Iris germanica L.

Bay Tree

Laurus nobilis

Hildegard held laurel in high regard but provided few therapeutic details, as if its benefits were self-evident. Indeed, the bay laurel (*Laurus nobilis*), also known as Apollo's laurel, enjoys such renown that it scarcely needs advocacy.

In ancient Greece, laurel symbolized immortality, awarded as a victory prize, particularly when achieved through heroism and wisdom. This tradition gave rise to the laurel crown worn by heroes, sages, and geniuses. The Pythia and soothsayers burned laurel in Apollo's honor to enhance their prophetic powers. Those who received favorable omens often returned home with a laurel crown.

Laurel can grow as a shrub or tree up to 10 meters tall. Its lance-shaped leaves emit a balsamic aroma when crushed. Its whitish flowers, grouped in clusters of four to five, bloom in March and April. Male and female flowers grow on separate plants. Bay laurel leaves contain lactones and alkaloids, responsible for their bitterness, as well as volatile molecules that repel insects. Traditional Aleppo soap is made using laurel berry or leaf oil.

Laurel is also used medicinally. Crushed leaves are prized for treating severe migraines, with the powder inhaled as snuff. Laurel powder, typically made from dried leaves, is widely available in grocery stores. Dried flowers or young leaves brewed as an infusion relieve abdominal cramps.

Dried laurel berries share the culinary properties of the leaves and are grated like nutmeg. Laurel leaves are a key ingredient in bouquet garnishes for flavoring meats or fish in sauces. Fresh leaves are also used in broths, fish stews, or ragouts.

228. *Laurus nobilis L.*   **Lorber.**

Lavender

Lavandula officinalis

Hildegard also wrote: "If lavender is boiled with wine — or, if wine is unavailable, with water and honey — and drunk warm and often, it soothes liver and lung pain as well as chest vapors." This aligns with ancient traditions: lavender, as its name suggests, cleanses and perfumes. Depending on its use, it is highly disinfectant and repels lice.

Lavender, a quintessential Mediterranean plant, is a shrub with blue, mauve, or violet flowers arranged in spikes, most species being highly fragrant. True lavender (*Lavandula officinalis*) is antiseptic, anti-inflammatory, febrifuge, circulatory, digestive, tonic, and healing. It is used in dried flower form or as an essential oil. Lavender is a component of numerous remedies for respiratory issues and flu-like symptoms. Soaps, detergents, cleaning products, and cosmetics often use lavandin (*Lavandula intermedia*), which has a stronger scent.

Lavender is ideal for relieving headaches, soothing intestinal spasms, and warding off insomnia; flowers are often placed in pillowcases. For rheumatic pain, macerated lavender flower oil or essential oil diluted in vegetable oil can be massaged into the affected areas. To repel insects, lavender bouquets can be hung upside down throughout the house. A few sprigs in wardrobes effectively deter moths.

In the Nice region, a particularly potent lavender liqueur with digestive and calming properties is produced.

Lavender requires sunlight and calcareous soil. It also acclimates well north of the Loire River. Regular pruning of stems is essential to stimulate growth and harvest flowers.

79

Lentils

Lens culinaris

Hildegard tempers her disdain for lentils as food with the esteem she has for very hot poultices made from them, particularly in the case of scabies: *"Apply them to the wounds until the discharges stop and the patient recovers."* Scabies, which causes intense itching, is a parasitic skin disease caused by a tiny mite. Contagious through skin-to-skin contact, the disease is now cured with internal or topical treatments, often antibiotics. In the Middle Ages, treatments were limited; lentils, rich in vitamins A and B, as well as in minerals (calcium, iron, phosphorus, potassium, magnesium), could relieve and prevent infections related to scratching. Furthermore, the mite responsible for scabies is killed by high temperatures. Hildegard's advice, even if difficult to implement, is therefore not absurd.

Lentils have effects on the nervous, digestive (intestinal transit), and hormonal systems (irregular menstruation, menopause, prostate conditions). They contain essential amino acids that the body cannot synthesize. During the same meal, when one combines a legume (lentils, split peas, fava beans, beans, or chickpeas) with a cereal, the digestive system can reconstruct the necessary proteins.

To limit bloating, soak lentils for a whole night. After discarding the soaking water, cook them in fresh water over medium heat. From the beginning of cooking, you can add aromatics: garlic, rosemary, basil, chervil, bay leaf, sage, thyme, etc. Maintain a gentle boil for about twenty minutes.

In the garden, sow in spring in well-drained, light, and loose soil. Generally, they are alternated with cereals or leafy vegetables for perfect crop rotation. They are also used as green manure to be plowed under.

450. Ervum Lens L.   Linse.

Lupin

Lupinus luteus or *Lupinus albus*

There are hundreds of varieties of lupins. Hildegard refers more specifically to the white lupin, likely to discourage the harvesting of wild lupin. White lupin and "sweet" yellow lupin are cultivated and contain little to no alkaloids, unlike wild yellow lupin or "sulfur lupin," which is very toxic.

Lupin seeds consist of an outer coating, the tegument, which is a source of fiber, and an inner part, the cotyledons, rich in protein. They also contain carbohydrates, fats, and minerals. The composition of its fats is comparable to that of rapeseed. Its fibers are an excellent appetite suppressant and aid intestinal transit, making it a facilitator of weight loss.

In recent years, lupin beans have appeared as an aperitif snack. Orange in color, flat and round, they are enjoyed in brine, like olives, or dried and salted, like peanuts.

Lupin flour has a slight hazelnut taste. An alternative for gluten-intolerant individuals, it is ideal for reducing bad cholesterol. Combined with wheat flour, it enriches bread or pizza dough with protein. Vegans use it as an egg substitute in cake batter or mayonnaise, as it acts as an emulsifier. Allergies to lupin are rare and often linked to cross-reactivity with peanuts.

Its oil, with healing and anti-inflammatory properties, is a cosmetic for hair and facial care.

Gardeners are well-acquainted with this pretty flower, which sways its tall spikes up to 50 cm high. Colorful varieties integrate well into flowerbeds and rock gardens. Lupins prefer well-drained, sandy soils and do not tolerate shade. They make an excellent green manure, fixing atmospheric nitrogen and enriching the soil for subsequent crops.

LUPIN.

Mallow

Malva sylvestris

Hildegard also recommends the cooked flower for gastric pain and its dew, applied around the eyes, to brighten vision. In the Middle Ages, and since Antiquity, mallow was called *Omnimorbia*, meaning a panacea capable of curing all diseases, starting with respiratory ailments.

The plant blooms from May to September, multiplying its mauve flower heads, as its name suggests, on bushy, hairy stems that can reach over a meter in height. Its root is white, and its leaves resemble ivy leaves. It thrives near buildings and grows along paths, embankments, or ruins. Its fruits, shaped like small wheels of cheese, are called "cheeselets."

Mallow contains numerous active substances, but primarily mucilage with anti-inflammatory and soothing properties, known to calm irritated mucous membranes or skin. It also contains minerals and vitamins A, C, and B-group vitamins. Mallow tea is consumed to combat ailments of the oral sphere (coughs, sore throats, canker sores, bronchitis, and laryngitis), water retention, phlebitis, and gastrointestinal ulcers. It also relieves inflammation of uterine, bladder, or pyloric mucous membranes.

As a poultice made from leaves and flowers, mallow accelerates the healing of abscesses, ulcers, and wounds. Mallow is edible. Considered a vegetable since prehistoric times, it is eaten raw in salads or cooked in soups. In the garden, it is undemanding. You can sow "cheeselets" or replant cuttings, offshoots, or divided clumps. Be warned: once it takes to a spot, it can become invasive.

Malvaceae.
Malva silvestris L.
W. Müller n. d. Nat.

Melon

Cucumis melo

The varieties we have today are rounder, more fragrant, and sweeter than those Hildegard knew, which likely explains her lack of enthusiasm. It is unlikely that she cultivated them in her monastery gardens. Originally from intertropical Africa, the melon, in one form or another, has been grown as a vegetable since antiquity. During Roman times, it was the size of a quince, rare, and considered a luxury dish served with a spicy sauce. It was known in France up to the time of Charlemagne but was gradually forgotten for various reasons. It was only in the early sixteenth century, during the Italian wars, that it was reintroduced to this side of the Alps.

The melon belongs to the Cucurbitaceae family. Its leaves are broad and rounded. The flowers are yellow. There are several hundred varieties and sub-varieties, such as Cavaillon, Brodé, and Cantaloupe. It is a good source of vitamins A, B, and C. It is also rich in fiber and potassium, making it a very laxative food and useful for preventing kidney stones.

A good melon should have a pronounced fragrance (a sign of ripeness), be heavy (a sign that it is full of sugar), and have a stem that begins to crack or detach. It keeps better in a cool cellar than in the refrigerator. It can be eaten as a dessert or as a vegetable. It is enjoyed in sorbets, pastries, tarts, mojitos, soups, or salads. For instance, it pairs with lamb's lettuce and shrimp, accompanied by a sauce made with balsamic vinegar, honey, and lime. It is often served with avocado, goat cheese, or Parma ham. Almond and melon tart, citrus and melon verrine, champagne and melon cocktail, pork tenderloin with melon—it seems that this friendly cucurbit is a companion to all dishes!

In the garden, it needs a warm, sunny spot and well-manured soil. To grow beautiful melons, some precautions are needed, such as pinching off buds and removing leaves, but with a good gardening guide, it is not too difficult.

Melo sive Melopepo vulgò. Dod. 663 — Ital. Melone. — Gall. Melon
Melo vulgaris. T. 104.

Mint

Mentha piperita or *Mentha arvensis*

For most medicinal plants, it is necessary to be precise about the specific variety described, but this is almost impossible for mint, as varieties easily hybridize. However, pennyroyal (*Mentha pulegium*), with its hepatotoxic components, should be avoided.

In addition to pennyroyal and water mint (*Mentha aquatica*), Hildegard distinguishes between small mint, large mint, and Roman mint. The latter is today called spearmint (*spicata*). All mints have comparable properties. Peppermint (*piperita*), which is more potent, is used in phytotherapy.

Rich in menthol and flavonoids, mint is digestive, respiratory, hepatic, relaxing, antiseptic, and sudorific. It treats migraines, nausea, liver disorders, and rheumatism. Peppermint is reputed to reduce the effects of intoxication: nausea, imbalance, drowsiness, etc. Mint is not recommended for pregnant women or those with excessively heavy menstrual flow.

You can use mint in all your dishes: salads, meats, fish, pastries, or sorbets. With or without alcohol, there are numerous mint syrups, liqueurs, or cocktails. Infusions are consumed plain or blended with tea, verbena, ginger, or lemon.

Mints are perennials with white, pink, or bluish flowers. Easily recognized by their scent, their leaves are opposite, lance-shaped, and serrated. The seeds, often sterile, are difficult to sow. It is better to take cuttings by dividing the roots. Plant in the spring. You can also grow it in pots. Choose a semi-shaded location. Mint prefers fertile, cool soils. To stimulate growth and encourage the formation of new leaves, pinch off the inflorescences. It repels chiggers, aphids, and ants. Water at the base, never on the foliage, as it is sensitive to powdery mildew and rust.

Tip for migraines

Massage your forehead and temples with peppermint essential oil.

Mentha piperita L.

St. John's Wort

Hypericum perforatum

In the Middle Ages, St. John's wort, or herb of St. John, was used to heal wounds. It was also considered a protective plant against dark forces because, at that time, mental disorders (depression, anxiety, etc.) were often attributed to demonic possession. This flower, resembling a small sun, is particularly celebrated on June 24, St. John's Day. Originally, the solstice celebration was pagan, but ecclesiastical authorities moved this magical feast by a few days, as they did with Christmas. Large bonfires are lit in honor of St. John the Baptist, and it is also a celebration for future spouses. Each person wears a garland or carries a bouquet of St. John's wort.

The herb of St. John can grow up to a meter high. Its flowers have five bright yellow petals and long stamens. The leaves have tiny transparent vesicles, giving rise to the name *millepertuis*, meaning "a thousand perforations." St. John's wort grows in sunny areas, often along paths, embankments, or forest edges.

Endowed with antibacterial, antiviral, antiseptic, anti-fatigue, anti-inflammatory, and antidepressant properties, St. John's wort is also diuretic, febrifuge, and appetizing. Researchers have discovered xanthophylls (yellow pigments) and flavonoids in it, which act on dopamine and serotonin, regulating mood and sleep. The plant is recommended for insomnia, anxiety attacks, or mild depression.

Externally, it is soothing and healing. For wounds, poultices made of crushed fresh plants are applied. St. John's oil (recipe at the end of the book) soothes light burns and sunburns.

In garden centers, you will mostly find "improved" or hybrid St. John's wort. It is simpler to gather seeds of *Hypericum perforatum* from pathsides. Flowers are harvested from mid-June, and seeds in July.

Precautions

Do not take St. John's Wort while undergoing certain serious medical treatments (heart problems, cancer, HIV, etc.) or taking oral contraceptives. If in any doubt, consult your doctor.

Tüpfel=Hartheu, Hypericum perforatum.

Nutmeg

Myristica fragrans

The nutmeg tree is a Southeast Asian tree with clusters of yellow flowers that produces two spices: nutmeg and mace. Until the late Middle Ages, nutmeg trade was a secretive and exclusive domain of the Venetians. Today, nutmeg is cultivated worldwide but remains relatively expensive.

The phytochemical components of nutmeg give it antiseptic, antiparasitic, pain-relieving, neurotonic, and sedative properties. In high doses, it is hypnotic, hallucinogenic, and abortive. In low doses, it does not produce psychoactive effects. Mace is a red covering around the nutmeg, under its protective shell. It turns orange when dried. Ground into powder, it has medicinal properties similar to nutmeg.

Essential oils are easier to use medicinally because dosing is simpler. There are two types: oil derived from nutmeg itself and mace oil (more expensive). Both have similar properties but slightly different scents.

Grated and sprinkled, nutmeg enhances red meats, vegetable purées, cocktails, or desserts. It is used to flavor gratin dauphinois, Savoyard fondue, béchamel sauce, quiche Lorraine, and curry sauce. Mace, with its more refined taste, is preferred for zander, perch, white meats, or luxury chocolates.

Precautions

Essential oil, even for external use, is not advised for pregnant or breastfeeding women and children under seven years old.

Myristicaceae.
Myristica fragrans Houtt.

Common Barley

Ordeum vulgare

Hildegard advises against barley, whether cooked or cold, for both the sick and the healthy. However, there are two exceptions to this prohibition. The first is a daily bath in a barley maceration-decoction "for the sick who have already lost almost all their strength." The second is the use of a barley infusion as a lotion for people "whose facial skin is hard and rough and dries out easily due to wind."

Hildegard's distrust of barley is likely because the grain requires well-drained soil and a relatively dry climate to grow well and concentrate maximum nutrients, which is not commonly the case in Germany. Nevertheless, the benefits of barley for dry, eczematous skin or psoriasis have been known since ancient Greece. *Hordeum vulgare*, probably native to the Middle East, is one of the oldest cultivated grains and remains one of the most widely grown worldwide, from the Arctic Circle to tropical regions.

In the Middle Ages, barley was a grain for the poor, while the bourgeoisie and nobility ate bread made from wheat flour. Barley contains proteins, lipids, and vitamins B and E. It also provides essential amino acids, trace elements (selenium, phosphorus, iron, zinc, copper, magnesium), and gluten, which acts as an appetite suppressant. Barley is available as "hulled" grains (whole, with their hairs removed but retaining the bran) or "pearled" grains (polished and refined). Nutritionally, hulled barley is more beneficial. It can be consumed as flakes or flour. Barley grains can also be prepared like bulgur or rice. Sprouted grains are added fresh to salads, and dried grains are used to brew beer. Roasted barley grains can replace coffee in digestive and tonic decoctions.

Barley is sown in September and October for winter barley, which is very hardy, and in February and March for spring barley, which is more delicate and sensitive to cold. There are also decorative varieties for ornamental gardens.

Hordeum vulgare. L.

95

Nettle

Urtica dioica

There are several varieties of nettle. The most common are stinging nettle (*Urtica dioica*) and small nettle (*Urtica urens*), which have comparable properties and flavors. Hildegard recommends cooked nettle but also highlights its use in fresh juice form: "If memory is failing, crush stinging nettle to extract its juice. Mix with a little olive oil. Before bed, massage your chest and temples with it; forgetfulness will diminish." This excellent remedy is also effective for the whole body to relieve skin problems, as well as muscle or joint pain. Nettle is rich in silica, a structural component of our bones, ligaments, and tendons. Its hairs contain gallic, acetic, and formic acids, flavonoids, histamine, serotonin, and phytosterols. Thanks to its mineral and vitamin content, especially vitamin C, nettle is renowned for combating fatigue, circulatory and urinary issues, headaches, decreased libido, osteoporosis, hot flashes, constipation, migraines, and fever.

Everyone recognizes nettle by its heart-shaped, serrated leaves and, above all, its stinging hairs. Stinging nettle, which often grows taller than 1.5 meters, thrives in shaded areas or uncultivated land.

Along with dandelion, nettle is one of the best wild vegetables. Its flavor is mild. It is best harvested in spring when it is more tender. The tops, with or without flowers, can be cut (using scissors) throughout the year. For teas, dry your harvest in the shade.

To enjoy it in salads or as a vegetable, avoid soaking or wiping, as this would break the hairs and let the nutrients escape. A simple rinse and quick draining are sufficient. For salads, snip nettles directly into the dish using scissors. Drizzle with olive oil and vinegar to neutralize the stinging effect of the hairs. The salad will no longer sting. When cooked, nettles can be eaten like spinach or dandelion greens.

178. Urtica dioica L.   Große Brennnessel.

Sorrel

Rumex acetosa

Sorrel is a perennial plant with broad, elongated leaves. Hildegard distinguishes three varieties: meadow sorrel, black sorrel, and white sorrel. Modern translators and phytotherapists have difficulty identifying the exact plants she refers to. Hildegard specifies that the first is "beneficial for animals, but not for humans," which is likely meadow sorrel (*Rumex arifolius*). Later, she mentions white and black sorrel, which have comparable properties. Hildegard does not recommend any of the three as vegetables but as remedies for nervous disorders ("madness") or as a regulator for the menstrual cycle.

Scientific analysis presents a mixed view of sorrel. On the one hand, the plant is rich in minerals and vitamins, giving it undeniable digestive and laxative properties. On the other hand, it contains oxalic acid, which can bind calcium in the intestines or kidneys. It is therefore recommended to cook it twice, rinsing after each cooking, to remove as much oxalic acid as possible. It is also advised to avoid cast-iron cookware, as iron imparts an unpleasant taste to the leaves. Pregnant women should not consume sorrel as a precaution. It is also unsuitable for people with kidney stones.

By following these precautions, sorrel can be enjoyed. It pairs well with white meats or fatty fish. Who hasn't heard of sorrel soup or the famous recipe for salmon with sorrel?

Infusions made from fresh young leaves should be mild to avoid bitterness: a cup after meals will aid digestion. Sorrel gargles can relieve mouth infections or sore throats.

Sorrel is difficult to reseed, so it is best purchased in potted form. Plant it in spring or autumn and water regularly throughout the year. To promote leaf growth, trim flower stems as soon as they appear.

Tab: 145.
c a b d e
g f h
Rumex alpinus. L.

Parsley

Petroselinum hortense

Parsley is recognizable by its lobed, scalloped leaves with a distinctive aromatic fragrance, especially when crushed. Its umbrella-like flowers are greenish or whitish. The taproot is yellow and strongly scented. In the wild, care must be taken to avoid picking wild parsley (*Petroselinum crispum*), as it can be confused with fool's parsley (*Aethusa cynapium*), which is highly toxic.

In addition to vitamins A and C and various phytochemicals, parsley contains an essential oil rich in apiol, nicknamed "parsley camphor." It is a plant with restorative, diuretic, and lactation-stimulating properties. In Europe and warm countries, parsley has long been a traditional remedy, with its uses confirmed by phytochemists and ethnobotanists. Infusions of parsley leaves, used as eye baths, soothe conjunctivitis. Internally, the same tea aids digestion. Root decoctions are recommended for urinary system issues (infections, retention, or stones). Crushed parsley poultices relieve engorged breasts, burns, rheumatism, or insect bites.

As a condiment, parsley is used whole or more commonly chopped. It is added to sauces or dishes either during cooking or just before serving. Parsley is used to garnish fish, meat, or salads. A side of fried parsley makes an excellent accompaniment to saucy dishes. Some varieties have been selectively bred, especially in Germany, for their edible roots, which are used in stews or as side vegetables.

In spring, before sowing parsley in loose soil, soak the seeds in water overnight.

V.2. 102. Umbelliferae.
361 Petroselinum sativum Hoffmann.
Gemeine Peterſilie.

Dandelion

Taraxacum officinale

Did you know?

The latex applied gently to a wart daily will make it disappear. In case of irritation, rinse with clear water.

Hildegard does not specify which other foods should be combined with dandelion. It could be sage, plantain, or watercress, which she praises highly and which are delicious in salads mixed with dandelion leaves. Like a small sun, the dandelion blooms from April to September, and its seeds cluster into round puffs that scatter at the slightest breeze. Undemanding, it grows along paths, in fields, or in gardens. Its toothed leaves are delicious in salads, as are the flower buds. Its root reaches up to 50 centimeters into the ground. The latex in the stem or root is toxic if ingested in large quantities.

Rich in minerals, calcium, sulfur, and silica, dandelion is a strongly diuretic plant. It is also recommended for its circulatory, laxative, purifying, and digestive properties. It combats liver insufficiency, hypercholesterolemia, and rheumatic pain. It stimulates the appetite and sluggish livers. It protects the cardiovascular and nervous systems. Decoctions of dried roots eliminate urinary problems. This concentrated tea can also be used as a lotion to massage the joints or improve circulation in the legs.

Externally, dandelions are healing. Simply apply a poultice of leaves to small wounds.

For cooking, choose young dandelions, as the leaves become tougher, bitterer, and stringier as the season progresses.

In your garden, sow the achenes in spring after soaking them in water overnight. On loose soil, scatter a few seeds and press them lightly into the soil. Thin them out if necessary when the first leaves appear. Be careful to avoid letting your vegetable garden be overrun. You can also leave dandelions in the lawn and mow after harvesting and early flowering.

Compositae.
Taraxacum officinale Web.

Plantain

Plantago major, *Plantago media*
or *Plantago lanceolata*

Hildegard mentions plantain twice. First, she refers to African plantain or psyllium, which she rightly recommends for stomach pain. Its mucilage forms a protective layer that reduces gastric acidity. Second, she describes another variety, *Plantago*, which grows in meadows and is a favorite of cows. Hildegard provides more detail on this type of plantain, which is easily identifiable by its long, lance-shaped leaves, thick and arranged in a rosette. Whether it is broadleaf (major), narrowleaf (lanceolata), or intermediate (media), these three types of *Plantago* resemble each other and have comparable medicinal properties. They belong to the same family as African plantain (*Psyllium*) but do not share the same appearance.

Rich in pectin, flavonoids, tannins, sulfur, calcium, and other components, plantain has numerous benefits. Antiseptic and expectorant, it soothes coughs and helps combat bronchitis. It improves circulation and relieves tired legs. As a hemostatic and healing agent, it stops bleeding. Its soothing properties regulate intestinal transit. It is even an effective appetite suppressant: its seeds, consumed with plenty of water, swell without being digested, aiding intestinal transit. In teas, the leaves, flowers, roots, or seeds can be consumed throughout the day or used as an eye wash. In fact, pharmacies sell plantain-based eye drops, sparing you the trouble of making your own.

Applied directly to the skin, plantain relieves insect bites and stops bleeding.

Young leaves can be eaten in salads. If they are too tough, cook them lightly, such as steaming, like other leafy vegetables.

To grow plantain, sow seeds in spring and harvest in autumn. It responds well to division. Dry the leaves in the sun to make your own teas.

Precaution

Plantain pollen can be allergenic.

Prairies, lieux herbeux.   Bords des chemins, lieux incultes.
Fleurit d'avril en septembre.   Fleurit de juillet en octobre.

A. — **Plantain lancéolé.**   B. — **Grand Plantain.**
Bonne femme.   *Plantain des oiseaux.*
P'antago lanceolata.   Plantago major.
— PLANTAGINÉES. —

Leek

Allium ampeloprasum

"The leek causes anxiety during the pleasures of love in humans," reproached Hildegard. Regarding sexual matters, one might question the depth of knowledge possessed by a nun bound by a vow of abstinence. Her ambivalence about the nutritional value of leeks is all the more surprising given that the vegetable was among the recommended crops listed in the *Capitulare de Villis*, established under Charlemagne's reign two centuries earlier. For similarly puzzling reasons, Hildegard advised against leeks for the sick. For the healthy, she offered the following recipe: *"Soak them in wine with salt or in vinegar until they are sufficiently softened."*

The leek has long green leaves. Their base forms a white pseudo-stem called the "shaft." Among the many leek species, *Allium ampeloprasum*, the perennial leek, was cultivated in Hildegard's time. Today, there are several cultivars, including Oriental garlic, which is particularly appreciated by chefs. Consumed by humans since the Paleolithic era, leeks are featured in a Mesopotamian recipe — the oldest known to us.

The flavor of leeks lies between that of onions and asparagus. They can be eaten cold in a vinaigrette, but are more commonly used in hot dishes: quiches, gratins, soups, stews, fondues, or pot-au-feu. Leeks are also a powerful medicinal plant with disinfectant and digestive properties. The greenish-white flowers, grouped in umbels, are also edible.

In the garden, leeks prefer cool, deep, humus-rich soil and tolerate winter cold well. They are propagated in two stages: first by sowing and then by transplanting. Considering the need to conserve water resources, it is worth noting that perennial leeks (*Allium ampeloprasum*) require less watering than other varieties. They are also less susceptible to pests, making them easier to cultivate without pesticides.

11,1
14. Liliaceae.
3.
2.
A.
1.
4.
256. Allium Ampeloprasum L.

Pear

Pyrus communis

Hildegard provides a pear compote remedy to *"eliminate bad humors and purify man, just as one cleans a vessel of the filth it contains,"* and to alleviate migraines. This is one of her most comprehensive and famous recipes.

In her time, pear trees cultivated in France and Germany produced varieties such as the "pear of anguish," which were so unappetizing and astringent that they were only eaten cooked in wine, with fennel or coriander. They were also oven-dried. It wasn't until three centuries later that juicy and sweet pears emerged, enjoyed raw.

The pear tree, often grafted onto quince, can grow up to fifteen meters tall and live for two hundred years. Pears are rich in sugar and high in calories. They contain vitamin C, B-group vitamins, pectin, which slows the sensation of hunger, and insoluble fiber that regulates intestinal transit.

Pears are categorized as "dessert pears," "cooking pears," or "cider pears." When perfectly ripe, dessert pears are eaten with or without their skin. Peeled pears have antidiarrheal properties. The fruit and the leaves of the pear tree, often consumed as infusions, are diuretic.

As a dessert, pears can be enjoyed poached in syrup, roasted, in charlotte, crumble, tart with almonds, compote, mousse, or bavarois. The famous *Pear Belle Hélène* is a pear in syrup accompanied by a scoop of vanilla ice cream, whipped cream, and hot chocolate. *Poiré* is a lightly alcoholic, fermented pear juice. Pears are also distilled into brandy, the most famous of which is made from the Bon Chrétien or Williams varieties, introduced in the fifteenth and nineteenth centuries.

In orchards, pear trees can be trained against a wall to promote fruit ripening and simplify harvesting. After pollination and once the fruit has formed, it is advisable to bag the pears to prevent wasps from devouring them before you can.

Pera Campana

Ant. Serantoni disegno   Stef. Rinaldi incise

Peas

Pisum sativum

Hildegard feared that peas might exacerbate cold and moist illnesses, which primarily occur in winter and are associated with phlegm—one of the four humors that govern the human body. Nonetheless, her insightful advice reflects her understanding that peas restore strength and aid intestinal transit.

In the Middle Ages, peas were consumed with their pods. Although listed as a garden crop in Charlemagne's *Capitulare de Villis*, peas were mainly considered fodder plants or food for the poor during famines. It wasn't until the Renaissance that eating green peas became fashionable, and their true popularity emerged in the nineteenth century.

Throughout history, peas have been part of the pharmacopoeia. Applied as a poultice, they were used to reduce sprains and soothe dermatological issues like eczema or warts.

Tender and slightly sweet, green peas are rich in vitamins B, C, and E, as well as proteins and potassium. Their high fiber content makes them nutritionally beneficial for humans, though not for sheep or cattle. In vegetarian diets, they are a good substitute for meat when combined with grains.

"Smooth" peas are earlier varieties, while "wrinkled" peas are sweeter, larger, and stay tender longer. Fresh peas, whether boiled or steamed, are often served as a side dish with onions or carrots. They are also used in salads, mixed vegetable dishes, or purées. Dried peas or "split peas" must be soaked overnight before cooking.

Peas thrive in well-drained, loamy soil and prefer a warm, sunny location in spring.

XVII, 2. 106. Leguminosae.
453. Pisum sativum L. Brech-Erbse.

Chickpeas

Cicer arietinum

Unlike other plants for which Hildegard provides detailed recipes, she gives no further instructions for chickpeas. This is likely because chickpeas, cultivated in the Mediterranean basin, were relatively rare in medieval Germany. The domesticated chickpea (*Cicer arietinum*) closely resembles its wild ancestor (*Cicer reticulatum*). As a legume, like peas, beans, soy, lentils, clover, or licorice, chickpeas bear butterfly-shaped flowers at the ends of slender, vine-like stems. Most legumes play an important role in human nutrition.

The fruit of the chickpea plant is a small pod with glandular hairs that contains one to four seeds. Its cultivation thrives in dry soils and is excellent for crop rotation, particularly in the third year after durum wheat.

Chickpeas are high in vitamins B and E, carbohydrates, minerals, and dietary fiber. Most notably, they are rich in protein, making them an ideal complement to cereal-based or vegetarian diets. Their amino acid profile is nutritionally comparable to that of beef. Chickpeas also contain a biologically active isoflavone with powerful anti-inflammatory effects, making them beneficial for individuals with irritable bowel syndrome.

Raw chickpeas, combined with fava beans, are used to make falafel. Cooked chickpeas are found in culinary preparations like couscous or hummus. To cook chickpeas, they must be soaked overnight in water, ensuring they have three to four times their volume in water. Adding baking soda can make them softer and easier to digest. If soaked too long, chickpeas may begin to sprout.

Cicer Sativum. J. R. H. 389.
Ital. Cece rosso. Gall. Poids chiche.

Apple

Malus domestica or *Malus sieversii*

Hildegard speaks highly of the apple tree, which occupies the top position in the section on trees in *The Book of Divine Works*. She provides remedies made from leaves, buds, flowers, or fruits. While Hildegard's preparations are complex to make, their efficacy is notable: arthritis or rheumatism, eye or skin problems, and liver or bile issues.

Since antiquity, the apple has been considered the ultimate medicinal food. Modern science has proven that this fruit possesses remarkable circulatory, digestive, laxative, anticancer, and anti-inflammatory properties. Apples stimulate the brain, ward off migraines, protect the cardiovascular system, promote sleep, and may help prevent Alzheimer's or Parkinson's diseases.

As everyone knows, this fruit is packed with vitamins, minerals, and slow-digesting carbohydrates that help fight fatigue throughout the day. It also contains flavonoids—antioxidant compounds that aid in cancer prevention and slow aging.

Apples store well and can be eaten raw or cooked throughout the year. Naturally, only organically certified fruits should be consumed. Apple cider is also excellent for health and is considered an effective weight-loss aid. Apple pectin facilitates the gelling of jams and serves as an appetite suppressant in dietary supplements. Infusions of dried flowers or fruits are known to combat coughs.

In orchards, plant apple trees preferably during the waning moon. Winter pruning shapes the tree, removes dead wood, and clears away shriveled fruits. To prevent fungal diseases, bury garlic cloves at the base of the tree.

Pirus Malus L.

Purslane

Portulaca oleracea

Purslane has small, round, tender green leaves. Hildegard, describing it as "cold," advises against its consumption without further explanation. While it is true that purslane is a weed that spreads inexorably, this hardly justifies such mistrust! With its spicy and tangy flavor, purslane is a delightful addition to salads.

It is identifiable by its fleshy leaves. In summer, it produces small yellow flowers, and its creeping stems smother less hardy plants.

Purslane is a cornerstone of the Cretan diet, known for promoting longevity and health. This is primarily due to its fatty acids, which have antioxidant and cardioprotective properties. Its vitamin E and C content and balanced mineral composition (potassium, magnesium, and calcium) make it a diuretic and fortifying agent, earning its reputation as a "detoxifier." Low in calories and rich in water, it is recommended for weight-loss diets and for cleansing the digestive and urinary systems.

Externally, purslane leaves can be applied directly to the skin or crushed to soothe skin irritations, relieve muscle soreness, or ease cramps. Its flesh is moisturizing, soothing, healing, anti-inflammatory, and antibacterial.

Preparing purslane is extremely simple—just rinse it. Young stems and leaves can be eaten in salads, mixed into an omelet, or cooked like spinach. In Greece, purslane is fried in olive oil with feta, tomatoes, and garlic. Chewing a few leaves can reduce gum inflammation and even soothe sore throats.

Purslane grows spontaneously in warm regions. You can cultivate it in your garden as long as you control its spread. At the beginning of summer, sow on loose soil, cover the seeds, and water frequently but gently. Thin out overcrowded plants. Two months later, harvest the most appetizing shoots! Water after harvesting to stimulate new growth. The leaves should be eaten quickly as they do not keep for long.

226. *Portulaca oleracea L.*   **Gemeiner Portulak.**

Lungwort

Pulmonaria officinalis

Since antiquity, lungwort has been a prime example supporting the doctrine of signatures. The foundational principles of this theory, developed by Dioscorides, posit that a plant resembles the organ it is meant to heal. With its lung-shaped leaves featuring spots and veins resembling bronchi, lungwort was believed to have been created by God specifically to treat lung ailments.

Hildegard upheld this tradition and recommended lungwort for respiratory diseases. Remarkably, modern research has confirmed that its mucilage, tannin, and saponins make it emollient, expectorant, astringent, and diuretic. Thus, it is ideal for treating flu, coughs, colds, and bronchial congestion. Moreover, as a diuretic and antibacterial agent, it aids in toxin elimination and facilitates urination.

Currently, scientists are exploring lungwort extracts as a potential treatment for cystic fibrosis. Recent studies have also shown that aqueous extracts of *Pulmonaria officinalis* contain polyphenols, flavones, and proanthocyanidins—antioxidant compounds biologically active against neurodegenerative disorders.

Lungwort is classified on the "B list" of regulated plants and is officially available only in pharmacies under medical supervision. However, it can sometimes be found in herbal shops as a tea, either alone or combined with other respiratory herbs like mullein.

Fresh lungwort can be eaten as a vegetable. Its young leaves, with a flavor similar to comfrey, can be enjoyed in salads. Cooking in water or steaming softens its texture, making it less coarse on the palate. It can be added to ratatouille or soups.

In the garden, plant lungwort in shaded areas along walls, where it quickly covers the ground.

LUNGEURT, PULMONARIA OFFICINALIS.

Horseradish

Armoracia rusticana

Hildegard does not provide culinary recipes but instead prescribes remedies for those who are "strong and stout" or who "have an excess of phlegm." According to the theory of humors, "phlegmatics" suffer from an excess of lymph or water retention.

Hildegard accurately identified horseradish's purifying, digestive, bactericidal, and stimulating properties. It is also effective against rheumatism and respiratory conditions like colds and sinusitis. This plant, with its large, shiny green leaves, belongs to the crucifer family, like mustard, and is primarily used as a condiment. It has a strong, spicy, peppery flavor, but unlike chili or mustard, the spiciness in the mouth fades quickly. Horseradish aids in the digestion of fats and, being very rich in vitamin C, acts as an energizer. In the Middle Ages, horseradish was a staple in gardens because it helped preserve food.

Horseradish remains popular in eastern France, Germany, Anglo-Saxon countries, and Eastern Europe, including Russia. It enhances sauces, fish, and meats. In Italy, horseradish is used in dishes like the beef stew *bollito misto* or the omelet *rafanata*. The leaves can be eaten raw in salads or cooked like spinach. If your intestines, stomach, or kidneys are sensitive, avoid overconsumption of horseradish, as it may worsen irritation.

Cultivating horseradish from seed is often challenging. Seeds are sown in early spring directly in their permanent spot, preferably in partial shade. Harvests are rare in the first year. It is easier to replant root fragments with buds. Horseradish slurry can be sprayed to combat fruit rot and seedling damping-off. It is also effective against powdery mildew and peach leaf curl. Planting horseradish at the base of fruit trees helps protect them from fungal diseases.

Cochlearia Armoracia
303

Rosemary

Salvia rosmarinus or *Rosmarinus officinalis*

In monasteries, rosemary holds a prominent place, much like mint, thyme, or bay leaf. It is a major remedy that Hildegard does not mention directly, perhaps because, botanically and medicinally, it is similar to sage or savory (*Bohnenkraut*). According to Hildegard's terminology, these "warm and dry" plants are first-line remedies for respiratory infections, arthritis, or digestive disorders.

Like savory and sage, rosemary grows wild around the Mediterranean basin but can acclimate further north, such as along the Rhine, in "parish gardens" sheltered from the wind. In Provence, its flowers—blue, white, or mauve—bloom from February to June. Fresh or dried, this aromatic herb is used in many dishes. Its honey, a specialty of Narbonne, is particularly renowned. Alongside rose and lavender, rosemary is one of the most common flowers in perfumery.

Rosemary has strong hepatobiliary, antispasmodic, and disinfectant properties. It aids digestion, relieves coughs and bronchial congestion, and is effective against flatulence, fatigue, and both physical and mental exhaustion. It is consumed as an infusion of leaves or flowers. Combined with cloves or savory, it is a key ingredient in mulled wine. Rosemary essential oil, particularly potent, is recommended for diffusion in a room or inhalation. A few drops in a bath stimulate blood circulation and help lower blood pressure.

In cooking, rosemary is used fresh or dried. Its flowers have a milder flavor and can be used to decorate cakes or ice cream. Its stronger-flavored sprigs enhance stews, soups, sauces, marinades, or grilled dishes.

In the garden, plant rosemary in a sunny location with calcareous, well-drained soil. It tolerates frost and benefits from light pruning after flowering. It multiplies easily in autumn through cuttings, division, or layering.

Rosmarinus officinalis L.

Blackberry

Rubus fruticosus

The bramble weaves its thorny stems up to 5 meters long into an impenetrable tangle. It should not be confused with the mulberry tree (or silk tree), which is rarely found in the wild and does not have thorns. The bramble's flowers are white or pink, with numerous stamens. Its red fruits, called "mûrons," turn black by late summer.

Once again, Hildegard is correct: the blackberry (or *mûron*) from the bramble is a marvelous medicinal food. The fruit has so many beneficial properties that you should feel no guilt when enjoying a blackberry tart freshly made from your harvest! It is an excellent hormonal regulator, recommended by Hildegard for painful or irregular menstruation. It also regulates sebum production. Tonic and antibacterial, blackberries reduce weeping dermatoses, dry patches, and eczema.

While fresh blackberries may not always be available due to their seasonality, and excessive consumption is not advised due to their sugar content, blackberry leaf and flower teas are an excellent alternative.

In season, blackberries can be eaten fresh or used in tarts, sorbets, or mousse. Blackberry jams keep for two years. For infusions, dry leaves and flowers (a pinch) are steeped in simmering water for two to three minutes. They have the same properties as the fruits. Decoctions of dried roots are used as skin or hair lotions. As gargles and mouth rinses, they relieve sore throats, pharyngitis, gingivitis, and toothaches.

If you have a large plot of land, plant brambles as a living hedge alongside hawthorn and holly. It will deter intrusions while providing refuge and food for birds and small mammals. Be warned, however: once a bramble takes hold, it is nearly impossible to remove. Prune it regularly to prevent uncontrolled spreading.

22.928
Reward
W.D. Irwin
Eckington D.C.
J.G. Passmore
Oct 9. 1901

Rose

Rosa gallica or *Rosa arvensis*

Hildegard is entirely correct! Rose-based eyewashes have been renowned since antiquity, and rose extracts for skincare are equally famous. In the Middle Ages, the rose was a powerful symbol, representing Mary, which is why its remedies were considered almost divine and why it inspired the magnificent rose windows in cathedrals. Legend has it that Thibaut, Count of Champagne, brought the Damask rose (*Rosa damascena*) back to Provins upon his return from the Crusades in 1254. However, botanists and historians agree that the so-called "rose of Provins" is identical to *Rosa gallica*, which was already common in Europe long before the thirteenth century. Thus, it is certain that Hildegard knew and used cultivated roses (*Rosa gallica*) as well as wild field roses (*Rosa arvensis*). For remedies or jam recipes, either type can be used interchangeably, as their medicinal properties are similar.

From the rose, not only perfumes and essential oils are extracted, but also various remedies. Rose infusions and rose water were commonly used as eyewashes and lotions until the last century. Rose syrup and honey treated headaches and stomach discomfort. Compresses made from petals, decoctions of red roses, and rose vinegar were used to relieve migraines, sore throats, mouth ulcers, intestinal pain, liver problems, and heart palpitations.

Its essential oil hydrates and regenerates dry skin, promotes healing, and soothes the heart, nervous disorders, asthma, and high blood pressure. Rose-based products are expensive because up to 10 kg of petals are required to produce just 5 ml of essential oil.

Wild roses (*Rosa arvensis*) and old garden roses (*Rosa gallica*) are the only truly nectar-rich varieties. They are planted between January and April and require sunlight and well-drained, neutral soil.

Did you know?

Rose hips, the fruits of the dog rose (*Rosa canina*), another variety of wild rose, are best harvested after the first frost. They are used to make jams.

Rosa Gallica Pontiana.

Rosier du Pont.

Sage

Salvia officinalis

In a detailed chapter on sage, Hildegard describes specific conditions it can treat: bad breath, arthritis, paralysis, limb pain, anemia, headaches, indigestion, bloating, incontinence, food poisoning, and other toxic exposures. Once again, Hildegard's insights align with sage's reputation as a panacea since antiquity.

Common around the Mediterranean and as far north as the Loire, sage is a pretty shrub with blue or violet flowers. Its thick, evergreen leaves emit a strong, characteristic aroma when crushed.

Sage is antibacterial, respiratory, digestive, liver-stimulating, analgesic, anti-rheumatic, calming, and antidepressant. It helps alleviate various pains and infections. However, it is contraindicated during pregnancy and breastfeeding. Women with cancer should avoid sage due to its phytoestrogen content. Its essential oil, which can be convulsive and abortive, is sold only in pharmacies.

With a slightly camphoraceous flavor, sage complements meats in sauces or stews, fish, pasta, and vegetables (eggplant, turnips, tomatoes, zucchini). Sage flowers can be enjoyed fried in batter and are also used to flavor pastries and sorbets.

For infusions, steep briefly in boiling water. Use an enamel pot and a wooden spoon, as iron alters the flavor and properties of the flower.

In the garden, sage requires sunlight, rocky soil, and minimal care. Once established in a suitable spot, it thrives and remains there.

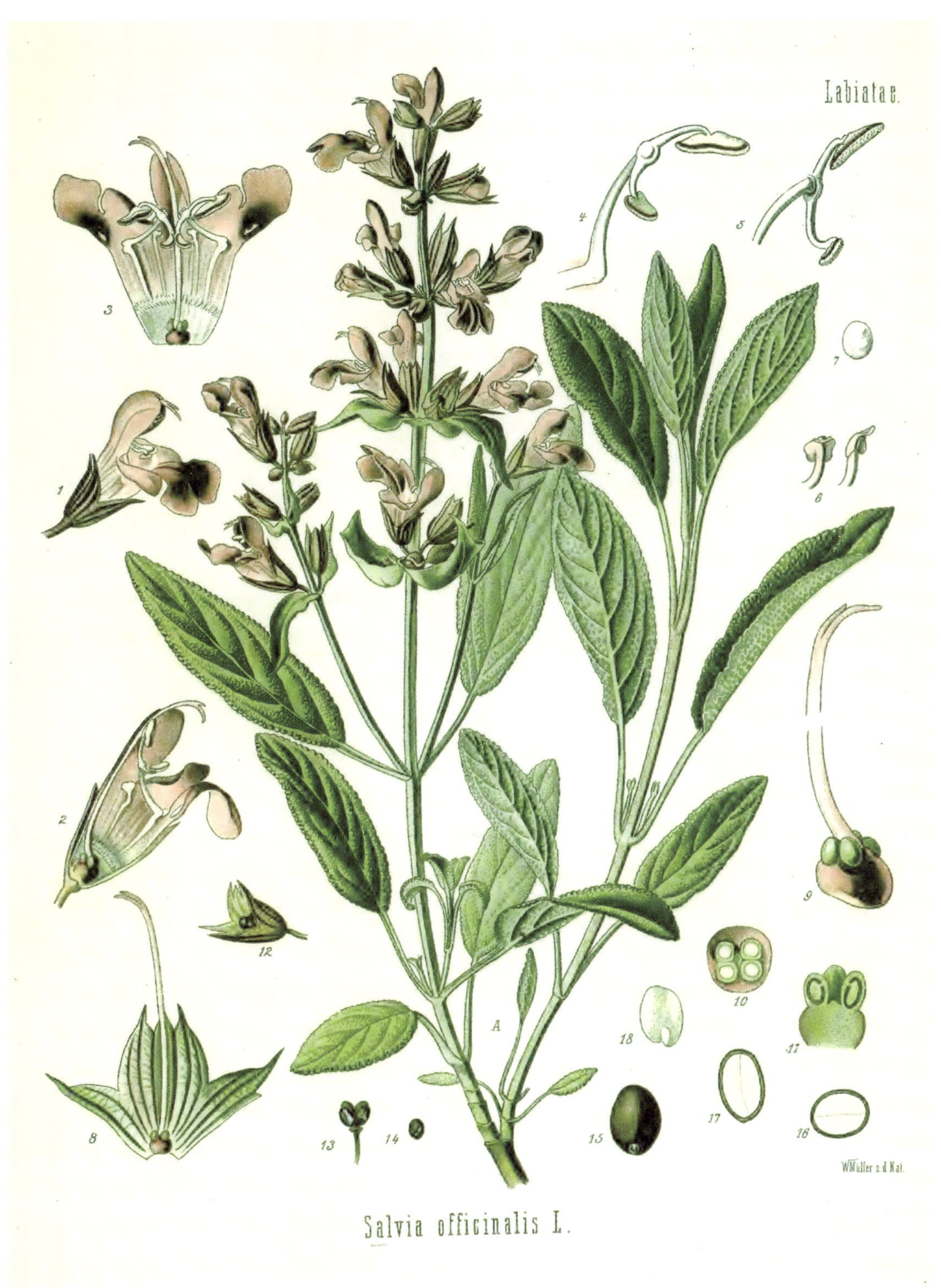

Salvia officinalis L.

129

Marigold

Calendula arvensis

The treatment Hildegard recommends continues with the ingestion of warm marigold wine, which induces vomiting to expel the poison. Today, in cases of toxic ingestion, one goes straight to the nearest hospital emergency room. In Hildegard's time, poisonings were common—whether intentional, to eliminate a rival, or accidental, due to ingredient confusion.

Etymologically, *souci* (French for marigold) means "the one that follows the sun," as its yellow flower heads turn toward the sun, mirroring it. Antispasmodic, hormonal regulative, healing (both internally and externally), hepatoprotective, and diaphoretic, marigold is a wonderful ingredient for medicinal preparations. Hildegard understood this well and, besides her anti-poison recipes, recommended creams for flaky skin (eczema) or scalp problems. Marigold lends itself to preparations made with beeswax and olive oil, particularly effective for eczema, acne, burns, or bruises.

Infusions are made from whole flowers (one per cup) or petals (5 g). Drink 3 to 4 cups daily for menstrual pain, liver issues, or digestive problems. Decoctions of the roots (20 to 30 g in 1 liter of water) make excellent soothing lotions for the skin or hair rinses. Petals can also be eaten as a salad garnish or used to decorate desserts.

Marigold is easy to cultivate, preferring well-drained, even dry, and sunny soil. Sow directly into the ground from April to September. Harvest the flower heads and dry them in the shade for teas. Pruning stimulates the growth of new flowers but leaves a sticky residue on your fingers. To prevent powdery mildew, use preventive treatments with horsetail manure or baking soda. Control its spread, as it can become invasive.

Calendula officinalis L.

Thyme

Thymus vulgaris

Hildegard does not elaborate on the description of thyme but provides detailed guidance on its uses, such as treating leprosy. This dreaded disease began to spread after the First Crusade. In the Middle Ages, doctors often treated leprosy with thyme fumigations or decoctions. These practices may have been somewhat effective, as leprosy is primarily spread through the upper respiratory tract.

Thyme is a branching sub-shrub with woody stems, small green leaves on top, and grayish undersides. Its flowers are white or pink, forming terminal clusters. A staple of European and Mediterranean pharmacopoeias, thyme is notable for its concentrated and diverse phytochemical profile. Its leaves and flowers are primarily used in infusions, essential oils, or alcoholic extracts. Thyme is a broad-spectrum anti-infective, antifungal, antispasmodic, analgesic, and immune stimulant. It also has circulatory, expectorant, and digestive properties, making it suitable for headaches, bronchitis, pain, rheumatism, and one of the best plants for relieving menopausal symptoms.

Externally, thyme disinfects wounds and treats fungal infections. However, it should not be applied to mucous membranes, as it can be harsh. There are several types of thyme essential oils, with the most potent being thymol-rich, which must be used cautiously.

Depending on the variety, thyme may have a hint of lemon or verbena flavor. It enhances all meat, fish, and vegetable dishes. Thyme is sown and transplanted in spring in full sun.

Labiatae.
W.Müller n.d.Nat.
Thÿmus vulgaris L.

Linden Tree

Tilia platyphyllos or *Tilia nobilis*

For Hildegard, the linden tree is a protective tree. She recommends its roots, sapwood, or leaves for heart disease, arthritis, or eye problems.

The linden tree is recognizable by its heart-shaped leaves and winged flowers (bracts) that appear in early summer. Their sweet scent perfumes the air and attracts bees. The flowers contain mucilage, tannins, flavonoids, and aromatic essence. Antispasmodic, diuretic, anti-inflammatory, soothing, and sudorific, they are ideal for promoting sleep, reducing mental fatigue, and alleviating digestion-related nervousness.

The sapwood, the inner bark between the outer bark and the wood, is particularly rich in phenols, tannins, and amino acids. Decoctions of sapwood act as a diuretic and detoxifier for the urinary system and are beneficial for the liver and gallbladder.

In April, young leaves, just sprouting from the buds, can be eaten. Tender and soft, they are a delightful addition to salads.

Linden products are available in pharmacies and herbal shops in many forms. Infusions of flowers, more fragrant than those of leaves, can be consumed throughout the day, preferably until late afternoon to avoid nighttime awakenings. Concentrated sapwood decoctions, consumed at a rate of one liter per day for three weeks, can help eliminate kidney stones and urinary insufficiencies. This decoction also serves as an excellent lotion for cleansing the skin and removing blemishes.

Plant linden trees in the fall. They thrive in sunny locations with deep, cool, calcareous soil. Young trees should be staked and weeded at their base.

TILIA platyphyllos.   **TILLEUL** à larges feuilles.   *pag.* 226

P. J. Redouté pinx.   Duruisseau Sculp.

Valerian

Valeriana officinalis

Catnip (*Nepeta cataria*), also recommended by Hildegard, is, like valerian, a plant beloved by cats and was widely used in the Middle Ages for respiratory ailments.

Valerian (*Valeriana officinalis*), also called "cat herb" or "St. George's herb," has clusters of irregular pink flowers. Its thick root divides and penetrates moist soil. Long renowned as a sedative, anxiolytic, and hypnotic, valerian is a natural alternative to synthetic medications for promoting sleep and alleviating anxiety. By relaxing the respiratory system, it is also beneficial for lung conditions.

Valerian's unpleasant smell, appealing to cats, is caused by volatile compounds responsible for its calming properties. For convenience, it can be consumed in various forms: dried root, alcoholic extract, essential oil, or tincture.

Root infusions are drunk an hour before bedtime. To experience its relaxing effects, add a concentrated root decoction to bathwater. Unlike synthetic sleep aids, valerian does not cause grogginess upon waking.

Valerian use is contraindicated for children under twelve and is not recommended for pregnant or breastfeeding women.

Sow valerian in the spring; it grows well even in cracks between stones. A garden variety exists with a milder odor and brighter flowers.

LÆGE-BALDRIAN, VALERIANA OFFICINALIS

Violet

Viola odorata or *Viola rupestris*

Hildegard draws a connection between depressive states and respiratory oppression. In the Middle Ages, violets were also considered aphrodisiacs and were slipped into pillows.

Viola odorata is a delicate winter flower with five violet petals, one of which has a spur. It spreads across meadows and gardens. The captivating scent of the sweet violet slightly numbs olfactory receptors, requiring a few minutes before the fragrance can be detected again. While used in perfumery, only the leaves are distilled. "Violet flower" scent is produced using synthetic molecules.

The flowers and leaves of sweet violet are expectorant, calming, sudorific, laxative, detoxifying, and diuretic. They are used for respiratory infections, rheumatic pain, nervousness, stress, and insomnia. The plant also relieves certain digestive symptoms. However, its reputation for treating asthma, epilepsy, or eczema may be overstated. Decoctions applied as compresses or added to bathwater soothe rheumatic pain, calm nerves, and reduce insomnia.

Young leaves, rich in vitamins A and C as well as minerals, can be eaten raw in salads or cooked in soups, where their mucilage thickens the broth. Fresh or candied flowers make beautiful decorations for pastries.

In the garden, violets are sown or transplanted in spring or autumn.

Precaution

It is not recommended to consume the roots, as they cause spasms and vomiting.

Grow, Multiply, and Harvest

et us take full advantage of the benefits of the best plants recommended by Hildegard. This is all the easier today, as we now know the actual properties of plants and their contraindications. The favorable environment for cultivating them, as well as the methods of preparing teas, medicinal wines, poultices, and other recipes, are also more familiar to us.

The Medicinal Garden (*herbularius*)

Monasteries, including Hildegard's, maintained a garden for medicinal plants (or *herbularius*). Even the ancient Greeks and Romans cultivated herbs in dedicated spaces. This idea was later adopted by Charlemagne, who published the *Capitulare de Villis*, a list of vegetables, herbs, and fruit trees required on imperial estates. Copies of this remarkable treatise have survived, providing valuable information on ninety-four varieties of fruits and vegetables. The organization of these gardens was highly precise: herbs were grouped in the *herbularius*, vegetables in the *hortus* (vegetable garden), and fruit trees in the *viridarium* (orchard).

Upon reading the *Capitulare de Villis*, one notices that the plants largely correspond to those described by Hildegard: sage, marigold, rosemary, cumin, chickpeas, melons, mint, parsley, celery, carrots, garlic, walnut, hazel, apple, pear, chestnut, peach, quince, almond, mulberry, laurel, fig, and so on.

Your Garden Plan and the First Planting

Before embarking on the creation of your *herbularius* (or medicinal garden), it is essential to design its layout and plan the placement of the various plants. The size will depend on the number of people who will benefit from it (beyond mere decorative purposes) and the number of individuals available to maintain it. In a monastery, where monks tend the garden in shifts throughout the day, these gardens can be quite large, especially if they are meant to provide not only medicine and food for all the monks but also for people from outside the community. For four people, however, it is better to keep the garden modest in size. There is no point in allowing it to fall into neglect, with overgrowth and invasive weeds. Garden beds measuring 2.5 to 3 meters on each side, with paths about 0.7 meters wide, are more than sufficient. The total area would thus be between 25 and 40 square meters, of which 20 to 25 square meters would be "usable," accounting for paths and hedges. Beds smaller than 1.5 meters on each side may create other issues, such as shading between plants, difficulty working the soil, or challenges with cross-pollination.

The medicinal plants in the *herbularius* are typically arranged into four thematic and geometric sections, often squares, corresponding to the four apostles who wrote the Gospels: Mark, John, Luke, and Matthew. Occasionally, a fifth central bed is added, encroaching on the corners of the other squares, in honor of the Holy Spirit, the Virgin Mary, or St. Paul, regarded as the thirteenth apostle. If this central space is dedicated to the Virgin Mary, it is often designed as a circle. Each section also symbolizes one of the five senses: taste, touch, smell, sight, and hearing.

The medicinal plants are arranged not only according to these symbolic criteria but also based on their practical uses (for fevers, digestive problems, women's ailments, etc.). This square-based plan allowed for the "classification" of medicinal herbs by their properties (diuretic, digestive, sedative, etc.). It is challenging and not strictly necessary to apply every possible criterion to each bed, such as the symbolism of the senses, the correspondence to illnesses or anatomical functions, the theory of humors, colors, and so forth. The most important consideration is to respect, as much as possible, the affinities between plants (see below, section "Friendly and Enemy Plants").

Some medicinal gardens are arranged in interconnected squares and diamonds, forming elaborate patterns that resemble a labyrinth—a symbol of humanity's difficulty in reaching paradise. Successfully creating such a masterpiece is also an extraordinary challenge!

The garden beds are bordered with trimmed boxwood hedges or hazelwood *plessis* (woven fences). The soil, mixed with compost, is mounded within each section,

Proposed implementation

Boxwood or woven willow fence

* *Plant to be isolated in a partially buried basin*

creating tiers that enhance the aesthetic appeal, improve sun exposure and drainage, and allow for easier access without the need to bend down or overreach. Pathways arranged in a cross pattern provide access and facilitate drainage. The palisades help break up drafts and limit cross-pollination between botanical varieties of the same family.

Boxwood, with its evergreen foliage, symbolizes the immortality promised to those who follow Christ's teachings. Among

Examples of Gardens

the most common plants are many of those described by Hildegard: fennel, lavender, parsley, rosemary, rose, sage, thyme, and others. Violets and marigolds can be scattered throughout to cover the soil and add splashes of color; these plants repel diseases, attract pollinators, and do not cast shade on their neighbors.

To contain the spread of certain plants (such as mint, sorrel, St. John's wort, nettle, and plantain), you can plant them in tubs buried three-quarters of the way into the ground. The same precaution applies to brambles, which can be controlled by planting them in deep containers.

It is not necessary to include all of Hildegard's plants in your *herbularius* — in fact, this would be quite difficult to achieve. Choose plants based on your preferences and their colors. Feel free to switch things up from season to season, according to your mood!

Friendly Plants, Enemy Plants

Each plant emits phytochemical compounds that strengthen its natural defenses. If a plant senses competition (often from another of the same family), it will find ways to eliminate the "rival." Therefore, it is essential to plant different varieties near each other.

- **Garlic, shallot, onion:** away from asparagus, marigolds, peas, cabbage, and beans, but near strawberry plants.
- **Beet, horseradish:** far from asparagus and spinach, but near beans, onions, salads, and savory.
- **Celery:** far from the other umbellifers (parsley, carrot, dill, angelica), but close to cabbages, cucurbits (melon), beans, and other legumes.
- **Carrot:** far from beets, horseradish, and mint, but near cabbages.
- **Cabbage:** far from garlic, fennel, leeks, radishes, and other cruciferous plants, but near celery, peas, borage, salads, spinach, mint, and beans.
- **Cucumber, pickle, squash, zucchini:** far from radishes, but close to basil, cabbage, fennel, beans, radishes, onions, asparagus, chives, and dill.
- **Bean:** near strawberry plants, carrots, and cabbages.
- **Lettuce:** far from parsley and near spinach, horseradish, beans, peas, and radishes.

- **Turnip and radish:** far from the other cruciferous plants, but near peas, lettuce, and spinach.
- **Parsley:** far from lettuce, but near cabbage.
- **Peas:** far from garlic, onions, leeks, fennel, but near asparagus, celery, and carrots.
- **Marigold:** near cabbage, lettuce, as well as at the bases of fruit trees and rosebushes.

If you are willing to deviate from Hildegard's logic by planting vegetables unknown in her time, note that tomatoes and eggplants should be planted near lettuce but kept away from potatoes, cucurbits, and peas.

Celery Cultivation

In the wild, celery grows in damp places. In the vegetable garden, both leaf celery and celeriac are grown using more or less the same methods. Sowing takes place from April to June in small pots, in a warm and well-lit room. Leaf celery is transplanted once, while celeriac is transplanted twice into pots of different sizes. The final planting is done around the end of April when they have six to eight leaves. Trim the tips of the small roots and the main root. Because celery requires plenty of organic material, adding compost is recommended.

Plants for Every Illness

Medicinal plants are more effective dry than fresh, as their phytochemical compounds are revealed and concentrated during the drying process. They should therefore be harvested and dried in the shade. Below is a brief glossary of ailments and the plants that alleviate them:

- **Headaches:** Chamomile, basil, lavender
- **Circulation:** Garlic, nettle, plantain, grapevine
- **Depression:** St. John's wort, gentian
- **Diabetes:** Cabbage, black radish, artichoke, olive leaves, nettle
- **Digestion:** Basil, cabbage, nettle, sorrel, black radish, rosemary, mint
- **Hypertension:** Olive leaves, garlic
- **Urinary infections:** Cherries, linden bark
- **Male libido:** Rosemary, nettle
- **Female libido:** Sage, angelica, nettle
- **Skin:** Burdock, wild pansy, plantain, carrot
- **Respiratory problems:** Basil
- **Rheumatism:** Willow, lemon peel
- **Sleep:** Hawthorn, basil, nettle, sorrel, linden, valerian
- **Stress:** Hawthorn

❧ The Preparation of the Soil

Soil that is turned by a rototiller or spade is depleted. It becomes overly compacted, draining poorly. Choose the Surface Cultivation Technique instead, or "SCT," which involves these four stages:

- From October to early January, cover your vegetable or medicinal garden with rather thick mulching (grass clippings, bark, hay).
- Remove this mulch and put it in the compost bin in the spring.
- Scrape the soil. Sow or install your plants.
- Mulch again. Do this superficially to keep weeds at bay without damaging the germination of your seedlings.

❧ The Soil

In order to accelerate the growth of your plants, you can enrich them with soil. Never use compost or manure directly at the base of your plants, as they are too nitrogenous. The soil is made up of so much fermented compost or manure that it is transformed into a homogenous soil. The right planting soil must be mixed with sand to enrich it with silica. Your seedlings need to be sieved.

❧ Seedlings

Some plants are sown, which is the case for most vegetables and herbaceous plants. For aromatic plants, vines, and shrubs, it is easier to propagate them by cuttings or layering. Seeds can be collected in the wild, exchanged with friends or neighbors, or purchased from garden centers. In the latter case, make sure they are medicinal or wild varieties, as indicated in Latin on the packet. You will sow them in seed trays.

✎ Transplanting

Wait for two or three leaves to appear before you transplant your plants. Water them and let them drain. Dig up the seedlings by pulling them very carefully by the leaves.

✎ Two Important Rules

- Alternate rows of cucurbits (cucumbers, squash, melons) and cruciferous plants (cabbages, radishes).
- Never plant cruciferous plants on the same plot for two years in a row. The same goes for nightshades (potatoes, tomatoes, and eggplants).

✎ Make Your Own Seeds

To ensure you use only organic or wild plants, make your purchases from trustworthy sources. At markets near natural parks, professional foragers often offer not only bags of plants but also seeds for replanting. Once acclimated to your vegetable garden or a rocky corner, medicinal herbs can be used regularly. To preserve future harvests, produce your own seeds. Mark a few healthy plants with a piece of wool—those with regular flowers and disease-free leaves. Water the base of the plants before and during flowering. Reduce the number of capsules, seed pods, or seed cases forming. Wait for the natural opening of the seed receptacles and harvest on a dry, sunny day. Immediately transfer the harvest onto absorbent fabric. Discard any broken, stained, or abnormally colored seeds. This technique works well for seeds of parsley, marigold, lettuce, fennel, St. John's wort, and dill.

❧ Propagation by Cuttings, Layering, and Division

Many shrubs and perennials (plants that do not require sowing every year) propagate effortlessly, almost as if multiplying like loaves of bread: a piece is taken, and it regrows. These techniques work well for plants such as mint, bramble, ivy, aromatics (rosemary, lavender, thyme, sage), hyssop, valerian, heather, roses, or nettles. Some plants tolerate multiple techniques equally well.

❧ Cuttings

Cuttings are taken between late spring and early autumn. Label the plants and note the date—this information is helpful for tracking rooting progress. Indoor plants, roses, and aromatics (rosemary, sage, thyme) are easily propagated this way. Cut a stem with two or three leaves (but without flowers) and place it in a vase filled with water for one or two months. Regularly top off the water to compensate for evaporation. Replant once the stem has developed a sufficient number of roots.

❧ Layering

Layering is suitable for plants with thick stems (such as marjoram, rosemary, or mint). Select flexible stems around the plant that can be bent to touch the soil. Remove the leaves at the point of contact. Secure the stem to the ground with a bent wire shaped like a staple or a heavy stone. Straighten the tip of the stem and tie it to a short stake inserted into the soil. Roots will begin to form after two to threemonths. Wait six months before separating the new plant from the mother plant.

❧ Division

Division works well for tubers, shrub roots (such as brambles and aromatics), chives, fennel, sorrel, mint, and succulents (such as aloe). Simply detach a portion of the roots or a sucker (a shoot growing from the base) and replant it. Moisten the plant before beginning. Water the mother plant and the newly replanted offspring generously.

❧ The Harvesting of Simple Herbs

Gathering plants in the wild is not prohibited, except for protected species, which are generally found in specific areas (such as nature parks or state forests). During a hike, it may be tempting to pick flowers because they are beautiful or because you think you can use them to make tea. However, do not take any risks! A good knowledge of botany is required to distinguish between two similar plants.

If you collect wild plants, never remove the roots. If you are unsure about their identification, consult an herbalist or a pharmacist. Additionally, wild plants may be contaminated by pesticide spraying, even if they grow far from cultivated areas. Avoid uprooting any isolated specimens, and be moderate in the quantity you gather. Harvesting seeds (pods, capsules, etc.) to replant in your garden is a more respectful practice.

Do not confuse hemlock with wild carrot!

Plants are identified by their flowers, stems, leaves, and roots. Mentioned in this book, fennel, angelica, anise, dill, green anise, chervil, parsley, and wild carrot all display lovely white or pink umbrella-shaped flower clusters (umbels) and a knotty, often ridged stem. They belong to the Apiaceae (or Umbelliferae) family. Rich in essential oils and resin—hence their antimicrobial, anti-inflammatory, and neurotoxic properties—Apiaceae plants are aromatic (and often used as condiments). This family also includes celery, parsnip, coriander, and cumin. Hemlock, which is highly toxic, is also part of it. Wild chervil (Anthriscus sylvestris) is very common. Its root is toxic and abortive. In spring, it covers embankments and roadsides with its white flowers.

Highly toxic umbellifers are hairless, though this does not guarantee that the hairy varieties are always edible. The rare exceptions shouldn't send you to the cemetery or even the hospital. For the most dangerous ones, such as hemlocks, crushing the leaves releases a strong odor of cat urine, whereas edible umbellifers give off the delightful fragrances that define them.

✌ Dehydration and Preservation

Vegetables are best eaten as fresh as possible, but medicinal plants are typically used dried, with a few exceptions. Drying, always done in an airy environment, alters the molecular structure of the plant and concentrates its active compounds. Dried plants also have the advantage of being consumable for up to a year or two. Do not exceed two years of storage in a sealed paper bag.

As a general rule, roots or thick stems should be dried in the sun, while leaves and flowers should be dried in the shade. Here are some guidelines for drying aromatics and medicinal plants:

- Form bundles of about a dozen stems, preferably with the most blooms (which are richer in active compounds). Hang them upside down in a warm, airy, odor-free space (not in the kitchen).
- For mixed elements or flowers alone, lay them out on a fine cloth or mesh.
- Store thoroughly dried herbs and flowers in glass jars or paper bags—never in plastic. Keep them in a cool, dry, and preferably dark place.
- Roots can be stored in sand or a cellar, protected from light, or wrapped in cloth and kept in the vegetable drawer of your refrigerator.

✌ The Moon

"From the heavens, the moon is connected to humans in every action of their lives; this is true for blood and humors, which are set into motion in tandem with the moon's movement."

Hildegard, in *Causes and Cures*, describes the interdependence between human beings, the celestial bodies in general, and the moon in particular: "In all humans, blood increases and decreases according to the waxing and waning of the moon. This applies equally to men and women."

151

The moon exerts its influence on Earth through measurable physical forces. These forces are not constant and vary according to the moon's movements. The physicist Isaac Newton demonstrated this, notably through the law of universal gravitation. For instance, tides are entirely correlated with the lunar cycle. Why, then, would the moon not also affect vegetation, which is predominantly composed of water?

Farmers who pay close attention to their crops follow certain guidelines. Simplifying somewhat, seeds are typically sown during the last quarter or just at the full moon, and harvesting is preferred during the first quarter, after the new moon. During highly disruptive periods such as the full moon, new moon, or perigee, it is advisable to wait a day or two. This is all the less problematic as lunar transitions often coincide with weather changes.

PART 3

Health Remedies and Kitchen Recipes

Ingredients That Hildegard Recommended or Advised Against

Hildegard sometimes provides recipes that are highly complex to prepare, involving ingredients that are now unavailable, such as parts of wild animals, or ingredients that no translator has been able to identify. Moreover, Hildegard rarely specifies quantities for even the simplest recipes. For her, the key lies in the ingredient—usually a plant—and the duration of the treatment, which should continue "until the patient is cured." Certain ingredients frequently appear in her recipes: spices (notably pepper, cloves, and galangal), wine, vinegar, honey, salt, olive oil, and, more rarely, milk.

✿ Bearwort (*Athamanticum*) or Mountain Fennel (*Mutellina adonidifolia*)

The root of the plant known as "bearwort" is regarded by some authors as the true medicinal chervil and thus the one Hildegard would have favored. It forms a dense clump of hollow, striated stems, and its leaves are divided into fine strips. It can be found throughout the mid-range mountains of Europe, from the Ardennes to the Massif Central. Cows love it, which contributes to the flavor of certain cheeses (such as Cantal, Saint-Nectaire, and Beaufort).

The dried seeds are used like caraway. The leaves, with their aniseed flavor, are used to season raw vegetables, salads, fish, and even meats. If you find it at markets, you can use it just like common fennel. All health or culinary recipes can be prepared interchangeably with either type of fennel. In Bavaria, a spirit called Bärwurz is made from the root of mountain fennel.

❧ Butter

> "If you suffer from asphyxia or coughs, or if your body is dry, eat butter. It heals and cures the sick. Butter is good for healthy people whose flesh is balanced. But if you are overweight, you have to eat it in moderation so as not to swell the diseased flesh."

In Hildegard's time, butter was difficult to produce, low in fat content, and quick to go rancid. It was therefore rare, relatively expensive, and preserved with added salt to prevent spoilage. Butter was not highly regarded by physicians, who generally preferred vegetable oils, such as olive oil, or animal fats like goose, beef, or pork fat, which kept longer. Today, butter is often spread on bread or added to steamed vegetables to enhance their flavor. However, frying or cooking with butter should be avoided, as its fats break down into toxic compounds at temperatures above 260°F.

❧ Lemon

Although Hildegard does not mention lemons in her writings, she was likely familiar with them. After the First Crusade (1096–1099), this delightful citrus fruit gradually spread through Provence and was carried further north by merchants. In some regions, its yellow color was associated with infamy. Lemons were not eaten as fruit but added to meat dishes to enhance their flavor.

Using Hildegard's logic, we could argue that lemon has "a good warmth" and is "moderately moist," which makes it effective against fevers. It extends the shelf life of foods, destroys germs on prepared dishes, and serves as an antifatigue, diuretic, antibacterial agent while protecting the cardiovascular system. Like vinegar, it seasons salads, accompanies meats and fish, and can be incorporated into cakes, jams, sorbets, or pies. Fresh lemon juice is perfect for dressing salads. If using the zest, wash the lemons and scrub them to remove preservatives. Preferably choose untreated or organic lemons.

❧ Cloves (*Syzygium aromaticum*)

> "Clove is very warm. It also contains a form of moisture that spreads gently, much like the gentle moisture of honey. If one suffers from headaches so severe it feels as though the head is breaking, or if one feels almost deaf, eating cloves frequently is beneficial."

Hildegard also recommends cloves for treating dropsy of the viscera (intestinal swelling and disorders), arthritis, and stuttering. This peppery, highly aromatic spice has a symbolic significance in religious history, representing the nails used in the Crucifixion. Emperor Constantine I is said to have gifted cloves to St. Sylvester, Bishop of Rome.

Clove possesses antibacterial, anesthetic, and antiseptic properties. Its high concentration of essential oils causes a burning and numbing sensation. Scientists have recently demonstrated that one of its components is effective against herpes. Clove is also used to relieve dental pain and neuralgia. Its bold, woody, and fruity flavor enhances dishes such as gingerbread, Biscoff cookies, marinades, sauerkraut, pot-au-feu, and curries.

Fenugreek (*Trigonnela foenum graecum*)

"Fenugreek is more cold than hot. Use against daily fevers that cause the patient to sweat and feel nauseous at the sight of food."

Hildegard recommends warm wine (the same recipe as with plantain) for fevers and limb pain. She also mentions bandages soaked in wine with fenugreek (see the section on poultices). Belonging to the Fabaceae family, also known as legumes, fenugreek is both a medicinal and culinary plant. Its seeds emit a caramel-like aroma, and their bitter flavor resembles celery. In the Middle Ages, the plant was believed to prevent hair loss.

Fenugreek has antifungal properties (against mycoses), acts as a laxative, and reduces cholesterol, making it an excellent spice for weight-loss diets. In cooking, fenugreek, alone or combined with other spices, pairs well with starches. A mix of coriander, cumin, and fenugreek creates delicious sauces for fish, seafood, curries, tagines, cassoulets, and lentils. Use one teaspoon for four people or a pinch per person.

Galangal (*Alpinia galanga* and *Alpinia officinarum*)

"Galangal is entirely hot. It contains no cold. It is full of virtues. If one burns with fever, drinking spring water with powdered galangal will reduce the burning fever.... If one has a sick heart, eating galangal quickly and in sufficient quantity will bring relief."

In this quote, Hildegard emphasizes "spring water," as water drawn from villages or streams was often contaminated. Galangal, to which Hildegard dedicates an extensive chapter, appears in many of her recipes. This aromatic spice, derived from a rhizome closely related to ginger, originates from Southeast Asia. There are at least two varieties, likely conflated in Hildegard's time.

- **Greater Galangal (*Alpinia galanga*):** Known for its aphrodisiac properties, it is thought to stimulate female libido. It is prized for its spicy, peppery, and slightly citrusy flavor. It stimulates appetite, aids digestion, and, thanks to its essential oil content, has antiseptic and expectorant properties. It relieves coughs, bronchitis, and sore throats.
- **Lesser Galangal (*Alpinia officinarum*):** With similar medicinal and culinary uses, it is rarer and more expensive. In the Middle Ages, it was only available in powdered or dried root form.

Olive

> "The olive tree is more warm than cold; it is a sign of mercy."

For Hildegard, the olive tree is a holy tree, as it is the most frequently mentioned plant in the Bible. During the Flood, the dove released by Noah returned to the Ark with an olive branch in its beak, a sign that it had found dry land. In the Gospels, Christ prayed in the Garden of Olives before His arrest and ascended to Heaven from the Mount of Olives. The Ascension remains a sacred and holy day in Christian tradition.

To treat arthritis or digestive problems, Hildegard provides several recipes for poultices made with olive leaves and bark mixed with lard. However, for both cooking and remedies, she prefers animal fats and advises against olive oil, stating that "it is not very good, as it can cause nausea and make other foods unpleasant to eat."

She does, however, recognize olive oil's healing properties for external use: "It has useful virtues for many medicines." She recommends vigorously rubbing the afflicted area with olive oil: "The warmth and strength of olive oil chase away the vapors of melancholy, and when massaged with the hand, the pain subsides." At the end of the text, several recipes for remedies are provided, including the famous "rose and violet oil."

Hildegard's criticism of olive oil is understandable, as medieval Europe was divided in its culinary preferences: Northern Europe favored cooking with animal fats, while

Southern Europe preferred olive oil. Today, olive oil is no longer bound by such regional distinctions. Its flavor has significantly improved, and its nutritional benefits are now widely recognized. Olive oil helps combat hypertension, bad cholesterol, and diabetes, while reducing the risks of breast cancer and cardiovascular diseases.

Contrary to a common misconception, possibly influenced by Hildegard, olive oil is easy to digest. It facilitates intestinal transit and stimulates the production of bile, which is released into the intestines.

Olive oil is suitable for both dressings and cooking, including frying, as its smoke point is much higher than that of animal fats and is the highest among vegetable oils. It is therefore possible to fry potatoes in olive oil, making them more digestible. The transformation of olives into oil can involve heating, the use of solvents, or cold pressing—the latter being preferable and clearly indicated on the label. Organic quality is also essential, as olive trees are susceptible to many diseases and pests. For dressings, oils with a protected designation of origin (PDO), such as the famous oil from Nyons, are recommended.

✢ Milk

Hildegard understood that milk produced in winter by cows eating hay is inherently less nutritious than milk derived from fresh grass. Today, it is difficult for urban consumers to access fresh milk straight from the cow. Fresh milk spoils easily and can carry diseases, leading to current regulations requiring refrigeration immediately after milking and, for large-scale distribution, potential pasteurization.

To reinvigorate winter milk, Hildegard advises adding "dried nettle root," stating, "the harmful humors in the milk are counteracted by the milk itself." Whether one is healthy or ill, Hildegard emphasizes that it is better to drink milk in moderation, regardless of the season, and recommends boiling it before consumption.

The overconsumption of milk and dairy products such as cheese or yogurt is relatively recent, spurred by the lobbying efforts of the agro-food industry. There is ongoing debate regarding the body's ability to process animal milk after childhood. Furthermore, the calcium in animal milk is said to be inferior to that found in many plants. Some studies suggest milk consumption may contribute to increased osteoporosis risks in Western countries. Additional criticisms include its hormone content, difficult digestion, bad breath, weight gain, and body odor.

After adolescence, milk is often recommended only in limited quantities, replaced with unsweetened, low-calorie beverages — spring water being the best option. However, can one truly forego a good pastry cream, caramel flan, vanilla ice cream, or quiche Lorraine? Such recipes are absent from Hildegard's works, but you will find a recipe for nettle milk a few pages later in the chapter on teas, soups, and other beverages.

❧ Honey

Hildegard discourages the consumption of honey as a food for both the "overweight" and the "thin": "It makes a person heavier. Melancholy grows within them." Honey was viewed as a potential indulgence, harmful to both body and soul. However, Hildegard also considers honey "as precious as gold," because its "gentle moisture" spreads through the body. While it should not be consumed regularly, honey is used as a remedy and features as a key ingredient in several recipes detailed later.

Honey has antiseptic, anti-rheumatic, and healing properties. It is also energizing, laxative, and tonic. In baking, honey can replace sugar, but adjustments are needed: it slows dough rising and increases baking time. Additionally, reduce the amount by about a third, as honey is sweeter than sugar. It is often better to use honey as a filling or glaze once the cake has been removed from the oven.

> **Honey tips**
>
> • *Minor burns or scrapes: after keeping the wound under lukewarm water for a long time, apply a thick layer of honey.*
>
> • *Facial "masks" and poultices with cucumber or cabbage can be enhanced with a thin layer of honey.*

❧ Egg

According to Hildegard, the egg is "more cold than hot and, regardless of its species, can cause severe harm; the egg is bad for health because it is slimy, viscous like a poison." However, she is more lenient toward the yolk of a chicken egg, provided it is cooked.

For those wishing to follow Hildegard's dietary principles, it is advisable to minimize egg consumption. This may be challenging for fans of pastries or Italian noodles. On the other hand, all other ingredients, especially spices, wine, and olive oil, can readily be incorporated into everyday cooking.

Pepper (*Piper nigrum* and *Piper longum*)

"Pepper is intensely hot and dry. It contains a wild force that can cause harm if consumed in large amounts.... If one suffers from the spleen and experiences aversion to the point of losing pleasure in eating, add pepper to a dish with bread."

Hildegard repeats this advice multiple times: in cases of difficult digestion, eat pepper. In the Middle Ages, spices like pepper were rare and prohibitively expensive, often used as currency. These dried plants, preserved to enhance their aromas, were primarily traded under the monopoly of the Venetians. During this era, long pepper was more commonly consumed, though it has largely been forgotten today. Its fruit consists of tiny seeds, with a warmer, slightly sweet, and less intense flavor than black pepper.

Whether black or long, pepper is rich in trace elements (potassium, calcium, magnesium, phosphorus, iron, manganese) and vitamins K and B. Most notably, it contains piperine, a molecule that aids digestion and boosts the production of endorphins, contributing to its reputation as an aphrodisiac. By stimulating gastric juice secretion, pepper improves digestion and is recommended for nausea, bloating, flatulence, or constipation.

Pepper also has pain-relieving and anti-inflammatory properties. As Hildegard mentions, it can alleviate headaches, joint pain, and muscle aches. It acts on the respiratory system, facilitating the expulsion of mucus, making it useful against bronchitis and colds. To relieve inflammatory pain, pepper is easier to use in the form of essential oil, which can be mixed with a vegetable oil (such as olive or sweet almond) for massaging the affected areas.

✑ Salt (Sodium Chloride)

"To eat food without salt cools the body's interior. Eating with
reasonable salting restores strength to a person and heals them.
Eating too much salt, however, dries out the body and causes harm."

Hildegard repeatedly advises against excessive salt consumption, particularly for those suffering from lung issues. While emphasizing moderation, she expresses a preference for *fleur de sel*, describing it as "useful for various applications and medicines, making remedies more effective when *fleur de sel* is added."

Salt, indispensable in small amounts, helps maintain healthy blood pressure and prevents dehydration-related complications. It also has positive effects on skin infections. In the Middle Ages, salt was scarce, taxed, and used sparingly. It was essential for preserving meats, fish, and some fleshy vegetables.

Modern salt consumption far exceeds what is necessary for proper bodily function. The average European consumes more than double the daily dose recommended by the World Health Organization. Today, salt is pervasive in processed foods, including charcuterie, cheese, and ready-made meals. This excessive and often unconscious consumption of salt has led to widespread epidemics of hypertension, cardiovascular diseases, and kidney disorders.

It is advisable to replace at least one-third of table salt with potassium salt or baking soda, both of which are alkaline and contribute to maintaining the body's acid-base balance.

✑ Medicinal Seeds (warm and cold)

In the Middle Ages, the seeds of certain plants were common ingredients in medicinal preparations. Called *semences* and likened in their virtues to human seed, they were categorized according to their warmth or coolness. These seeds were used to rebalance the body's humors by adjusting their hot/cold and moist/dry properties.

The four major hot seeds—anise, fennel, cumin, and caraway—relieve digestive issues. Among the cold seeds, chicory, lettuce, endive, and purslane are added to broths made with white meat to soothe agitation or anger.

Today, the use of medicinal seeds persists primarily in the form of the "tea of four seeds" (see the recipe a few pages ahead in the section on teas, soups, and other beverages).

✒ Wine

> "If it is pure, wine from the vine improves the blood of the one who drinks it. But if the wine is cloudy, it corrupts the blood, making it appear as if scattered with ashes."

Hildegard held deep reverence for the vine and wine, often incorporating wine, vine ashes, or leaves into the same remedy. She wrote,

> "The vine possesses the strength of fire and water, stronger than all other plants or trees.... If one has infected gums or sick teeth, add warm vine ashes to wine. Then use this wine to rinse the teeth and gums frequently to heal them."

Since Greco-Roman antiquity, wine has been a key ingredient in medicinal remedies, prized for its antiseptic, bactericidal, virucidal, and antifungal properties. It is also rich in vitamins, minerals, and other compounds with antidepressant qualities and benefits for the cardiovascular, digestive, and nervous systems. In the Middle Ages, wine was regarded as a panacea, a view reinforced by its role in Christian liturgy as the Blood of Christ. Wine was used to purify drinking water from wells or rivers, which were often contaminated by animal waste. Hildegard even mentions pollution of rivers caused by animal carcasses.

Her monastery, located on the banks of the Rhine, was surrounded by renowned vineyards. Hildegard especially praised wine from Hunsrück and advised diluting wine from Franconia. Wine was a staple at the table and a frequent ingredient in recipes. Hildegard also proposed wine-based treatments, such as dressings to soothe and heal skin ulcers.

However, wine in the twelfth century was quite different from modern varieties, as winemaking techniques were less refined. To preserve it, spices and honey were often added.

Today, wine remains a popular culinary ingredient. Opt for organic or "natural" wines. While it is enjoyable to pair wine with meals, one must be cautious: drink only sparingly and on special occasions, as it is well-documented that alcohol can cause more harm than good.

Hildegard offers dozens of wine-based remedies, including those made with wormwood, cinnamon, arum root, galangal, sage, parsley, and bay leaf. A dozen of her most well-known and effective recipes are detailed in the following chapter.

Vinegar

"Vinegar is good for all foods when added so as not to overwhelm the flavor and when its taste is not excessive. Consumed moderately with food, vinegar eliminates decay within the body, reduces humors, and allows food to pass directly through the body."

Hildegard preferred wine vinegar over cider vinegar, which she considered less digestible—likely reflecting the conditions of her time. Today, cider vinegar is highly valued for both its taste and its medicinal properties, which are often regarded as superior to those of wine vinegar.

Vinegar is formed through fermentation by the bacterium *Acetobacter*, which creates the "mother of vinegar" at the surface. This "mother" can be used indefinitely to produce new vinegar. Vinegar is disinfectant and antibacterial. When gargled or consumed in small amounts (less than half a glass per day), it alleviates sore throats, improves digestion, and soothes migraines and rheumatism.

Externally, Hildegard recommended dressings soaked in vinegar's "mother" to treat scrofula, also known as king's evil—a condition involving purulent fistulas caused by a form of tuberculosis. Scrofula was among the most severe and widespread diseases of the Middle Ages, alongside plague, smallpox, and leprosy.

Though scrofula has nearly disappeared, vinegar is still effective for treating pustules or boils. For insect bites or minor skin eruptions, apply a compress soaked in vinegar. Vinegar-based poultices can relieve muscle pain and stiffness in the neck.

In cooking, vinegar enhances sauces, mayonnaise, mustard, and marinades. Choose different vinegars—cider, wine, fruit, grain, flavored, or balsamic—based on your mood and the dishes you prepare.

HEALTH REMEDIES

Hildegard did not distinguish between remedies and culinary recipes. Often, instructions — lacking precise measurements — are embedded within a chapter on a specific plant. For practicality, I have grouped the remedies and recipes by category: medicinal wines, teas and soups, ointments and poultices, and cooking recipes. I have suggested safe dosages, replacement ingredients, or complementary ingredients where necessary to enhance efficacy or adapt flavors to modern palates.

The suggested dosages and cooking times for each remedy are indicative and should be adjusted based on the density of the plants, their maturity, or their concentration of essential oils.

❧ Medicinal Wines and Syrups

Plant-based wines are also known as "elixirs." Hildegard had a preference for wine-based remedies. Alcohol, after all, extracts more active compounds than water. This preference also stemmed from the undrinkable state of water in her time and the preservative properties of wine.

From my experience, I remain convinced — and this would not betray Hildegard's intentions — that it is possible to rely primarily on teas for healing and reserve medicinal wines and elixirs for crises or fevers. However, since this work focuses on Hildegard's remedies, medicinal wines naturally play a prominent role.

Derived from natural fermentation, wine itself is a concentrated source of phytochemicals and minerals, making it a remedy in its own right. Moreover, as a natural blend of alcohol and water, wine extracts both the water-soluble and fat-soluble active compounds from plants. Adding water (either before or after the infusion preparation) does not reduce the remedy's effectiveness and helps limit alcohol consumption.

Choose a high-quality wine, preferably "natural" or organic. Generally, red wines are favored for circulatory and digestive ailments, while white wines are better suited for detoxification, such as treating urinary infections or liver problems.

Never prepare wine-based remedies with uncoated metal utensils, as iron can alter the quality and properties of the preparation—especially for plants like sage or cinquefoil. Always stir with wooden utensils.

Medicinal wine should be stored in glass bottles, protected from light. For treatments lasting several days, refrigerate the wine between doses and reheat gently

Harvesting, an anonymous woodcut from the fifteenth century.

(without boiling) before drinking. Medicinal wines keep well for several months, even better than regular wines, due to the antimicrobial properties of the spices and herbs. In both the Middle Ages and antiquity, this was a common method for consuming and preserving wines.

As with teas (discussed below), the recipes for medicinal wines involve infusions, decoctions, or macerations.

- **Infusion:** High in alcohol, this is the least concentrated in active compounds. It is reserved for petals or plants with subtle fragrances.

- **Decoction:** The quickest and most common method. It allows alcohol to evaporate and active compounds to be extracted in a single cooking process. A brief boil (a few dozen seconds) is sufficient.

- **Maceration:** Preferably done in a sealed jar, either in sunlight or away from light, depending on local traditions. Macerations are mainly used for complex

168

recipes (involving multiple plants whose active compounds are to be combined) or for lotions treating pain or skin problems. The doses of plants and alcohol are higher.

For those mindful of their alcohol consumption, the following method can be used: prepare a decoction using only wine, boiling the plants in wine and allowing it to reduce so the alcohol evaporates. Then add water and reheat without boiling. The resulting elixir will not keep as well and will be slightly less pleasant to drink, but it will retain the same medicinal properties.

The concentration of plants is a delicate balance between flavor and medicinal potency. The doses provided in the recipes below are averages. Essential oil-rich plants (such as cinnamon, lavender, rosemary, sage) or spices (such as pepper, galangal) can render elixirs undrinkable if used in excess.

Medicinal wines and teas are rarely prepared with exact measurements. Generally, depending on the density of the leaves or petals:

- **2 g** corresponds to a small pinch (or ½ teaspoon of powder, such as galangal or pepper).
- **5 g** equals a regular pinch or one teaspoon.
- **10 g** corresponds to a generous pinch or one tablespoon.

❧ Galangal Wine

Ingredients

In a saucepan:

- 2 cups (½ liter) of red wine
- 2 cups (½ liter) of water
- Heaping ½ tsp (3 g) of powdered galangal (a generous pinch or more, if desired)

Preparation

Heat the wine in a saucepan, add the galangal, and bring to a boil.
Add the water and bring to a boil again. Remove from heat and let cool.
Drink one glass with each meal and one glass in the evening before bed.

❧ Cinnamon Wine

"For those paralyzed by arthritis," Hildegard provided a recipe involving "wood and leaves from the cinnamon tree while they still contain sap." Without traveling to Sri Lanka to gather fresh cinnamon leaves, one can still benefit from the spice by adding it (along with a pinch of pepper) to most warm wines. A pinch is enough to enhance the effects of galangal, lavender, or plantain wine.

❧ Fennel Wine

Hildegard of Bingen recommended this syrup for colds, fevers, or respiratory issues. It can also be effective in treating digestive disorders.

Ingredients

In a 2-quart or 1.5-liter glass bottle or jar:

- 6 cups (1.5 liters) of red wine, organic or natural
- 5 pinches of grated nutmeg
- 1 tbsp (10 g) of German chamomile
- 2 tbsp (20 g) of fennel seeds
- 1 to 2 tbsp (10 to 20 g) of ginger, minced into small pieces
- ½ to 1 tbsp (5 to 10 g) of rosemary
- ⅓ to ½ cup (5 to 7 tbsp) of honey

Preparation

1. Pour all the ingredients into the container and top off with red wine.
2. Seal the container.
3. Let macerate in the sun for about 10 days, shaking occasionally.

Drink morning and evening as a syrup. Do not exceed 6 tablespoons per day. Dilution with water is possible.

Contraindications: Not suitable for pregnant women, children, or individuals with epilepsy.

✐ Sage Wine

Ingredients

- 2 cups (½ liter) of red wine
- 2 cups (½ liter) of water
- 1½ to 2 tbsp (15 to 20 g) of sage

Preparation

1. Place the sage in the wine. Heat gently to a boil, then remove from heat.
2. Stir with a bamboo whisk or wooden spoon. Let cool to lukewarm.
3. Add the water and reheat until just below boiling.
4. Strain the liquid, preferably with a cloth or coffee filter. Avoid using metal utensils.

✑ Lavender Wine

"Lavender is warm and dry, and its warmth is wholesome. If lavender is cooked in wine — or, if wine is unavailable, with water and honey — and drunk often while warm, it soothes liver and lung pains, chest vapors, and grants clear understanding and a pure spirit."

Ingredients

- 2 cups (½ liter) of red wine
- 2 cups (½ liter) of water
- 1½ to 2 tbsp (15 to 20 g) of dried lavender

Preparation

1. Heat the wine with the lavender in a saucepan without bringing it to a boil.
2. Add the water and reheat until it begins to simmer.
3. Allow to cool and drink warm.

Store in a sealed bottle. Warm gently before each use.

✑ Plantain Wine

"If plantain is cooked in wine and this warm wine is drunk, it soothes high fevers."

Ingredients

- 2 cups (½ liter) of red wine
- 2 cups (½ liter) of water
- 1½ tbsp (15 g) of dried plantain, or 3 tbsp (30 g) of fresh plantain

Preparation

1. Heat the wine and water with the plantain in a saucepan without bringing it to a boil.
2. Allow to cool and drink warm.

Store in a sealed bottle. Warm gently before each use.

This recipe can also be prepared with fenugreek for similar issues, such as fevers or limb pain.

❧ Digestive Wine with Blessed Thistle

Ingredients

- 1 cup (¼ liter) of red wine
- 1 cup (¼ liter) of water
- ¼ cup (40 g) of blessed thistle seeds (or aerial parts)
- 2 tbsp (20 g) of dill

Preparation

1. Heat the wine and water with the plants in a saucepan without bringing it to a boil.
2. Let simmer for 2 to 3 minutes.
3. Allow to cool and strain. Optionally sweeten with a spoonful of honey.

Store in a sealed bottle. May be consumed cold or slightly warmed.

❧ Parsley Wine

"Parsley is more beneficial raw than cooked. It soothes mild fevers. If one suffers from heart or spleen issues, cook parsley in red wine with added honey."

Ingredients

- 2 cups (½ liter) of red wine
- 2 cups (½ liter) of water
- ¼ cup (40 g) of fresh parsley

Preparation

1. Heat the wine and water with the parsley in a saucepan without bringing it to a boil.
2. Allow to cool and drink warm.

Store in a sealed bottle. Warm gently before each use.

❧ Iris Wine

Ingredients

- 2 cups (½ liter) of red wine
- 2 cups (½ liter) of water
- 2 small iris rhizomes

Preparation

1. In a mortar, crush the rhizomes and gradually add the wine.
2. Heat the resulting mixture in a saucepan without boiling.
3. Depending on the thickness and difficulty of straining, add water as needed.

Drink warm. Store in a sealed bottle. Warm gently before each use.

Consume one glass morning and evening, alternating with a linden decoction. Store sealed in the refrigerator, and dilute with water and warm before each serving.

❧ Horseradish Wine

Hildegard offered two similar recipes against the retention of water, fatigue, and excess weight. She suggested adding fennel in the first recipe. She recommended adding galangal in the second one. But she did not give the proportions. The recipe below is similar to a horseradish sauce if you add fresh cream to make the mixture smoother and creamier.

Ingredients

- 3 to 4 tbsp (30 to 40 g) of horseradish (or 2 tbsp (20 g) horseradish and 1 tbsp (10 g) fennel root)
- 2 cups (½ liter) of Alsace white wine (or wine vinegar)
- 1 to 2 tsp of honey
- Scant ½ tsp (1 to 2 g) of galangal
- Salt to taste

Preparation

1. Finely grate the horseradish under a stream of water to reduce irritation (or blend it).
2. Heat the wine and honey gently for 3 minutes.
3. Add the horseradish first, then the salt and galangal. Remove from heat.

Store in a jar. This remedy-condiment improves after 2 days and keeps well when refrigerated.

Optional: Add cream to soften the mixture before use.

❧ Violet Wine

"Cook violets in good wine, filter with a cloth, and add galangal and licorice. Drink this potion to put an end to melancholy, restore joy, and clear the lungs."

Ingredients

- 2 cups (½ liter) of red wine
- 2 cups (½ liter) of water
- 1 to 1½ tsp (10 to 15 g) of dried violets (or double the quantity if fresh)
- A pinch of galangal

Preparation

1. Heat the wine and water with the violets and galangal in a saucepan without bringing to a boil.
2. Let cool and drink at room temperature.

Expectorant Elixir with Fennel and Chervil

"If one has coughing fits so severe that the chest becomes painful, take lovage, an equal amount of sage, and twice as much fennel as the other two combined. Add to good wine until the wine absorbs the flavor of the plants."

Ingredients

- Red wine
- 1.75 oz (50 g) of fresh chervil
- 2 tbsp (20 g) of sage
- 3.5 oz (100 g) of fresh fennel
- 1 to 2 tbsp of honey

Preparation

1. Place the plants in a glass jar.
2. Add the honey.
3. Top off with wine and seal. Shake well.
4. Allow to sit in the sun for about 10 days.

In winter, gently heat the mixture in an enamel saucepan without boiling.

This elixir, which is only for adults, must be consumed in moderation (a teaspoon two or three times during the day as well at bedtime).

✐ Hildegard's Theriac or German Theriac

A theriac is a medicinal preparation used as an antidote. This recipe addresses respiratory issues, fatigue, libido decline, depression, flatulence, digestive problems, and food poisoning or allergies. It is not suitable for pregnant or breastfeeding women, individuals with hypertension, or those with heart conditions. The roots are added in the form of powder or cut into small pieces. In general, the roots are used after desiccation (that is to say, dried).

Ingredients
- ½ tsp (2 g) of angelica root
- ½ tsp (2 g) of licorice root
- ½ tsp (2 g) of gentian root
- ½ tsp (2 g) of ginger root
- ½ tsp (2 g) of green anise seeds
- ½ tsp (2 g) of fennel seeds
- ¼ tsp (1 g) of galangal powder
- ¼ tsp (1 g) of cinnamon bark
- ½ tsp (2 g) of lemon zest
- 1 pinch (0.2 g) saffron stigmas
- ½ tsp (2 g) of myrrh resin (or 3 drops essential oil)
- 1 tsp (5 g) of natural camphor
- 2 cups (1.5 liters) of wine

Preparation

There are two traditions: maceration in strong fruit alcohol (e.g., cognac, plum, pear) or in red wine. The wine-based method aligns more closely with Hildegard's spirit.

1. Combine all the plants. Place them in a sturdy glass bottle.
2. Add the myrrh and camphor.
3. Pour wine into the bottle, leaving 1 to 1.5 inches (3 to 4 cm) of space from the top.
4. Cover the bottle with tulle instead of sealing it.
5. Let sit at room temperature (or in the sun) for at least 3 weeks, shaking occasionally.

Drink a small glass of theriac before or during meals. If too bitter or strong, dilute with water or add honey. Avoid other alcohol during the treatment, which should last no more than three weeks.

❧ Herbal Teas and Other Drinks

Avoid tap water, which can sometimes contain high concentrations of pesticide residues. Like Hildegard, we should prefer spring water. Today, it is available bottled. Choose one that is low in mineral content. Do not use aluminum or cast-iron saucepans; instead, opt for enameled steel and wooden utensils.

Drink 2 to 3 cups (up to 1.5 liters) a day, depending on the condition. For urinary infections and kidney problems, drink plenty. For insomnia, stick to 1 cup before bed. For chronic illnesses, regularity and consistency are more important than dosage.

How to Prepare an Herbal Tea

Infusions involve steeping delicate parts of plants (such as flowers, thin leaves, or light seeds) and aromatic plants (like rose, tea, linden, nettle, or sage) in water that has been brought to a boil but not boiled. The plant is left to infuse while the water cools. Stir the water with a bamboo whisk (as with tea) or a wooden spoon to oxygenate the infusion. Infusions can be reheated, but while their medicinal properties remain intact, their taste and aroma diminish. Using kettles or teapots helps keep the water hot for longer. The typical dosage is about 1 tsp (5 g, or a pinch) to 1 tbsp (10 g, or a generous pinch) of plant per 3 cups (¾ liter) of water. Dosage also depends on the density of the plant material: dried angelica is heavier than linden bracts; powder is denser (and thus heavier) than petals, etc.

Decoctions involve simmering plant material in boiling water for a few minutes. This method is used for roots, stems, or bark to extract the maximum amount of active compounds. It is particularly suited for plants used to cleanse the liver or urinary system. The typical dosage is about 1 to 2 tbsp (10 to 20 g) of plant material per 4 cups (1 liter) of water, reduced to 3 cups (¾ liter) by gentle boiling. Drink throughout the day. If fresh plant material is used, double the quantities.

Macerations involve soaking plant material in unheated water, wine, or a combination of both, usually in a glass bottle placed in sunlight for several days. This method is typically used for external remedies or medicinal wines and is most effective for plants rich in tannins and vitamins. Heating is possible before straining and consumption, but never boil the mixture.

Decoction-macerations concentrate active compounds for use in formulas. These are not recommended as their taste is rarely pleasant and their preparation requires a basic understanding of medicinal techniques.

❧ An Agrimony Decoction Against Nervousness and Mental Disorders

Ingredients
- 1.75 oz (50 g) of agrimony root or 2.5 oz (70 g) of aerial parts
- 4 cups (1 liter) of water

Preparation
1. Soak the agrimony in cold water for 10 to 15 minutes.
2. Heat gently until boiling, then let it simmer for 3 to 5 minutes.
3. Let cool, strain, and vigorously massage the head with the decoction, or soak a cloth in it and cover the head.

❧ An Agrimony Infusion and Herb Robert

Hildegard's formula against mucus or the excessive secretion of saliva is intended to be made into pills. These are little suet balls in which the powder of different plants is added. It is also possible to make pills or "homemade" tablets, but you must have a manual tablet pill press at your disposal. It is a tool that you find in specialized stores and on the internet. In this case, you use the plant powder, to which you add flour as a binder.

Ingredients
- ½ tsp (2 g, or a small pinch) of aerial agrimony parts
- ½ tsp (2 g, or a small pinch) of Herb Robert (*Geranium robertianum*)
- ½ tsp (2 g) of fennel seeds
- 4 cups (1 liter) of water

Preparation

1. Add the plants to cold water.
2. Heat gently until boiling, then turn off the heat. Stir with a bamboo whisk or wooden spoon.
3. Allow to cool, then strain using a cloth or coffee filter if possible.

The tea can be consumed throughout the day, even cold if stored in the refrigerator.

A Sage Infusion

"Whether it is raw or cooked, it is beneficial for the one who is weakened by harmful moods."

Sage is antibacterial, respiratory, digestive, liver-stimulating, analgesic, anti-rheumatic, calming, and antidepressant. It helps combat various pains and infections and regulates the menstrual cycle. Pregnant or breastfeeding women should avoid it as a precaution.

Ingredients

- ½ tsp (2 to 3 g, or a small pinch) of sage
- 4 cups (1 liter) of water

Preparation

1. Place the sage in the water. Heat gently until boiling, then turn off the heat. Stir with a bamboo whisk or wooden spoon.
2. Allow to cool. Strain using a cloth or coffee filter. Avoid metal utensils.

Do not use too much sage as it is potent; excessive amounts make the infusion bitter. This tea is particularly recommended for women, as it regulates the menstrual cycle. Men can drink it without worry, and sage also stimulates libido.

❧ A Nettle Infusion

Ingredients
- ½ to 1 tsp (3 to 5 g, or a pinch) of nettle
- 4 cups (1 liter) of water

Preparation
1. Place the nettle in the water. Heat gently until boiling, then turn off the heat.
2. Strain and drink.

The taste of the nettle infusion is not unpleasant, but rather ordinary. It can be combined with rosemary (1 tsp, or 5 g) to enhance flavor. It is a panacea and is particularly useful for accelerating healing and the calcification of broken bones.

❧ An Infusion of Two R's: Rose and Rosemary (*Rosa, Rosmarinus*) … and Bramble (*Rubus fruticosus*)

"Rose is useful in potions, ointments, and all remedies, which it improves even in small quantities."

Ingredients
- ½ tsp (2 g, a small pinch) of rosemary
- ½ to 1 tsp (3 to 5 g, or a pinch) of dried bramble leaves
- 1½ tsp to 1 tbsp (7 to 10 g, or a generous pinch) of dried rose petals
- 4 cups (1 liter) of water

Preparation
1. Place the rosemary, bramble, and rose petals in the water. Heat gently until boiling, then turn off the heat. Allow to cool.
2. Strain and drink.

This tea is very mild if not too much rosemary is used. It is digestive, anti-infectious, and laxative.

❧ Linden and Hops Herbal Tea to Relax

Ingredients
- ½ to 1 tsp (3 to 5 g, or a pinch) of linden (flowers and bracts)
- ½ to 1 tsp (3 to 5 g, or a pinch) of hops
- 4 cups (1 liter) of water

Preparation
1. Place the linden and hops in cold water.
2. Heat gently until boiling, then turn off the heat.
3. Allow to cool, strain, and drink.

This calming and slightly sedative tea is best consumed in the evening before bed. Be cautious with hops, known to be an anaphrodisiac (libido suppressant).

❧ A Linden Sapwood Decoction

This tea purifies the urinary system and is also beneficial for the liver and gallbladder.

Ingredients
- 6 cups (1.5 liters) of water
- 2 to 3 tbsp (20 to 30 g) of loose linden sapwood (or 3 to 4 small sticks)

Preparation
1. Place the linden sapwood in cold water.
2. Bring to a boil and maintain a gentle simmer for 2 to 3 minutes.

Drink the tea (approximately 4 cups (1 liter) will remain) throughout the day. If possible, leave the sapwood in the pot (unless transferring to a bottle to take with you), creating a decoction-maceration. It can be reheated and consumed warm.

❧ Digestive Herbal Tea of the Four Warm Seeds

In Hippocratic medicine, throughout the Middle Ages and up to the eighteenth century, the tea of the four warm seeds was used for abdominal pain, bloating, and flatulence. Green anise, coriander, caraway, and fennel are intestinal calming and carminative plants, meaning they help reduce intestinal gas.

Ingredients
- Green anise seeds
- Coriander seeds
- Caraway seeds
- Fennel seeds

Note: Ensure proper identification of the plants. For example, cumin can be confused with caraway. Some herbalists sell pre-mixed teas.

Preparation
1. Mix the seeds in equal parts in a container.
2. Add 1 tbsp (10 g) of the mix to 4 cups (1 liter) of cold water.
3. Heat until just before boiling, turn off the heat, cover, and let infuse for 5 to 7 minutes.
4. Strain and enjoy immediately after meals or throughout the day.

❧ Violet Infusion

Ingredients
- 1 tbsp (10 g) of dried violets
- 4 cups (1 liter) of water

Preparation
1. Place the violets in the water.
2. Heat gently until boiling, then turn off the heat.
3. Strain and drink.

This violet tea is fragrant and delicate. Use small amounts. It is ideal for combating indigestion, coughs, and nervousness.

❧ Barley Water

Applied to the skin or scalp, this lotion soothes eczema. Combined with lemon and honey, barley water treats respiratory infections.

Ingredients
- 2 tbsp (20 g) of hulled barley
- 4 cups (1 liter) of water

Preparation
1. Soak the barley in cold water for at least 2 hours.
2. Slowly bring to a boil, then let simmer for 10 to 15 minutes, stirring occasionally.

Variation for Bath Use
- Adjust proportions to ⅓ cup (60 g) of barley for ½ gallon (2 liters) of water.
- Repeat instructions as above.
- Pour the resulting mixture into bathwater without straining, but use a tulle cover to protect the drain from clogging.

❧ Nettle Milk

Hildegard recommends adding nettle root to milk to make it more digestible.

Ingredients
- 1 oz (30 g) of dried nettle root (or 1.75 oz (50 g) fresh)
- 4 cups (1 liter) of whole milk

Preparation
1. Cut the nettle root into small pieces.
2. Heat the milk gently with the nettle.
3. Allow to cool and strain.

Drink warm (one to two glasses per day). Store in the refrigerator for no more than 2 days. Reheat gently each time before drinking.

❧ Sage Condiment

"If one has lost the desire to eat, take sage, a smaller amount of chervil, and garlic. Crush everything with vinegar to make a condiment. Dip food into this condiment to restore appetite."

Ingredients
- 3.5 oz (100 g) of fresh sage
- 1.75 oz (50 g) of chervil leaves
- 1 garlic clove
- Wine vinegar

Preparation
Crush all the ingredients, adding the vinegar gradually to form a paste with a consistency similar to mustard.

✿ Powders

Powders are made from roots (such as angelica, horseradish, iris, or ginger) that have been oven-dried at a medium setting (below 160°F) or dried in the sun for a long time before being ground and sieved. Although less effective, powders can also be made from aerial parts (flowers, stems, leaves), as Hildegard suggests for sage. Powders can be compressed into tablets, added to wine or hot water, or used as a spice sprinkled onto dishes.

✿ Iris Root Powder

"The iris is warm and dry. All its strength lies in the root, which spreads its vigor into the leaves."

Ingredients

- 2 or 3 relatively young rhizomes (avoid overly hard roots)

Preparation

1. Clean the roots and cut them into thin slices.
2. Dry them in the open air on a clean cloth, in sunlight, for at least two months.
3. Grind the dried slices in a coffee or spice mill to obtain a powder as fine as possible.

This highly fragrant powder, known as orris root powder, is white or ochre in color. Until the seventeenth century, it was a common cosmetic for hair and skin, as well as a treatment to whiten teeth and soothe sore gums.

Modern pharmacies and perfumeries still sell orris root powder, but ensure it contains iris rhizome and no chemical or mineral additives (e.g., titanium dioxide, benzyl salicylate, mica).

Applications

- As deodorant, dry shampoo, or toothpaste: Use directly.
- For facial cleansing: Apply to a cotton pad, moistened with water, for gentle cleaning.

✌ Poultices, Ointments, Oils, Plasters, and Eye Drops

✌ Medicinal and Massage Oils

Medicinal oils are used to soften the skin, heal closed wounds, or soothe burns that have already calmed. To make them, let fresh plants macerate in a bottle of oil for at least 10 days, preferably in sunlight. Olive oil is often used due to its inherent curative properties. For a milder aroma, you can choose almond oil, apricot kernel oil, grape seed oil, hazelnut oil, or wheat germ oil. For quicker preparation, medicinal or massage oil can also be made by adding a few drops of essential oil, such as chamomile, lavender, rosemary, angelica, yarrow, basil, lemon, turmeric, parsley, or mint. Use sparingly, as quantity does not equate to quality.

It is important to apply or massage several times a day and in the evening before bed. Massage gently to ensure the oil penetrates the skin (and does not stain linens). On the following pages, you will find several medicinal oil recipes, including rose oil and St. John's wort oil.

✌ Poultices and Plasters

The principle of a poultice is to apply a thick paste to the painful area to facilitate an exchange through the skin between the added material and the body's interior. This paste typically consists of crushed plants, either alone or combined with other varieties. Poultices can be applied cold or warm. The plant material is often mixed with flaxseed flour to thicken it, making it easier to spread and keep in place under a cloth or bandage. Clay poultices are also common and may (or may not) include essential oils, depending on the therapist and the case. Poultices can be made from nearly any plant, as well as clay, fruits, algae, or vegetables.

Necessary Equipment
- A saucepan, mortar, cutting board, and wooden spoon.
- The chosen plants, or green clay mixed with essential oil of the selected plant.

Guidelines
1. Never reuse a poultice.
2. Avoid using aggressive essential oils on the skin (e.g., thyme or sage); always dilute and thoroughly mix with a vegetable oil.

3. For burns, the poultice should never be cold or hot — always lukewarm.
4. Never apply a poultice to an open wound or skin destroyed by burns.

Poultices and plasters are often confused, and their terms used interchangeably (this is true in our translation of Hildegard's advice). In some regions, plasters are considered thinner than poultices, made from finer or more liquid material. In others, plasters are thicker. The principle remains the same. Plasters may be applied without needing to be secured by a bandage.

Creams, Ointments, and Cosmetics

Olive oil and wax are ideal for making fine creams or ointments that absorb well into the skin. Instead of animal fat, as recommended by Hildegard, one may use — exceptionally in natural product preparation — petroleum jelly. Petroleum jelly is completely inert, stores well, has no odor, and does not enter the bloodstream. Homemade cosmetics should be stored in labeled and dated glass or ceramic containers in the refrigerator. For massages, all organic, cold-pressed vegetable oils are suitable, including hazelnut, almond, or apricot kernel oil. A few drops of your preferred essential oil can be added. Oils will keep for several months in a sealed bottle, away from light.

Important: Before applying to a large area, perform a patch test on your wrist to ensure no adverse reaction.

✆ Aloe Poultice

Hildegard's formula for respiratory problems is also recommended in the case of the flu or aches.

Ingredients
- 10.5 oz (300 g) of fresh aloe vera pulp
- 1¼ cups (30 cl) of olive oil
- 3.5 oz (100 g) of mint leaves

Preparation
1. In a wooden or granite mortar, crush the aloe vera and mint with a pestle.
2. Gradually add the olive oil while mixing.
3. Pour the mixture into a cast iron or enamel saucepan and heat gently, stirring continuously.
4. Allow to cool slightly. Wrap the aloe vera mixture in a clean cloth and place it warm (not hot) on the chest. Press occasionally.

✆ Fenugreek Plaster

Ingredients
- 2 cups (½ liter) of red wine
- 3.5 oz (100 g) of fenugreek seeds

Preparation
1. Heat fenugreek seeds in red wine without boiling.
2. Crush the seeds as much as possible in the wine.
3. Spread the mixture onto a bandage and soak it well. Wrap it around the legs or arms.

❧ Fennel Eye Poultice

Ingredients
- 3.5 to 7 oz (100 to 200 g) of fresh fennel
- 1 egg

Preparation
1. Crush the fresh fennel.
2. Separate the egg white from the yolk.
3. Mix the fennel with the egg white and apply to the eyes.

There is no reason why the yolk would be less effective than the white. The recipe can be modified by mixing the entire egg with the fennel. Hildegard also gives a similar recipe for an eye lotion using mallow petals.

❧ Parsley Eye Drops (for tired or swollen eyes)

Ingredients
- 7 oz (200 g) of fresh parsley
- 2 cups (½ liter) of water

Preparation
1. Steep the parsley in hot (but not boiling) water for 2 minutes.
2. Strain and soak cotton pads in the tea.
3. Place the pads on the eyes.

Alternative: For swollen eyelids, apply crushed parsley directly to the eyelids. Plantain leaves and flowers can replace parsley in the same proportions for an equally effective eye lotion.

∞ Mallow Poultice for Depression

"If melancholy afflicts the brain of a patient…"

Ingredients
- 7 oz (200 g) of fresh mallow flowers
- Olive oil

Preparation
1. Crush the mallow flowers in a mortar.
2. Drizzle with a small amount of olive oil.
3. Apply the preparation to the scalp and secure with a cloth.

∞ Vinegar Lotions for Rheumatisms and Aches

"Garlic tip: For aches and muscle pain, macerate the cloves
of three garlic bulbs in a liter of cider or wine vinegar
after peeling and crushing them. Strain before use."

Ingredients
- 3 to 4 garlic bulbs
- 4 cups (1 liter) of cider or wine vinegar

Preparation
1. Peel and crush the garlic cloves.
2. Let them macerate in the vinegar for at least a week, shaking the bottle occasionally.
3. Massage the painful areas with the preparation.

This preparation can also be swallowed: 2 tablespoons in a glass of water before each meal.

❧ Chervil Ointment

Ingredients

- 3.5 oz (100 g) of chervil
- 7 oz (200 g) of carrot root
- 7 oz (200 g) of cabbage
- 1 tbsp (10 g) of lard (or petroleum jelly)
- 2 tbsp (20 g) of beeswax

Preparation

1. Press the chervil, carrot, and cabbage to extract their juice. Weigh the juice.
2. Add an equal amount of lard or petroleum jelly.
3. Mix gently while heating, then add beeswax.
4. Remove from heat and continue mixing until the ointment is cooled and homogeneous.

Apply to irritated areas or superficial wounds until healed.

❧ Nettle Ointment for Memory Lapses

"When you go to bed, massage it into your chest and temples. Forgetfulness will be rarer."

Ingredients

- 7 oz (200 g) of fresh stinging nettle (leaves with stems)
- Olive oil

Preparation

1. Crush the nettle in a mortar.
2. Gradually add olive oil to form a paste.
3. Apply the paste to the scalp at night, secure with a cloth (or shower cap).

❧ Carrot Plaster for the Skin

Grated carrot or fresh carrot leaf poultices soothe burns, abscesses, recent wounds, leg ulcers, and boils.

Ingredients

- 3 large carrots

Preparation

1. Blend or grate the carrots.
2. Spread the mixture onto the skin and secure with a cloth or bandages.
3. Carrot leaves can be slightly crushed and used similarly.

Keep in place for up to two hours, then discard the poultice. Repeat two to three times daily.

❧ Rose Ointment

"When affected by cramps or paralysis, rub with this ointment and you will feel better."

This creamy ointment, softer than the rose oil remedy (next recipe), is used for cramps and muscle pain. It can also serve as a day cream. If a tingling sensation occurs, rinse with clear or lemon water.

Ingredients

- 2 tbsp (20 g) of rose petals
- 1 tbsp (10 g) of sage
- 1 tbsp (10 g) of lard (or petroleum jelly)
- 2 tbsp (20 g) of beeswax

Preparation

1. Infuse the rose petals and sage leaves in 2 cups (½ liter) of water. Let the mixture reduce without boiling, stirring regularly.
2. In a separate pan, melt the beeswax in the lard, stirring with a wooden spoon. Remove from heat.
3. Gradually add the infusion to the wax-lard mixture while stirring until it cools and solidifies into a creamy consistency.

Keep refrigerated in a small glass jar.

↝ Rose and Violet Oils

Hildegard further notes that this recipe is also effective for arthritis, headaches, and kidney pain. This oil is used for massages.

Ingredients
- 2 cups (½ liter) of olive oil
- 2½ tbsp (25 g) of dried rose petals (or ⅓ cup (50 g) of fresh petals)
- 2½ tbsp (25 g) of dried violet petals (or ⅓ cup (50 g) of fresh petals)

Preparation
1. Heat the oil in a double boiler or directly in a pan without boiling. Remove from heat.
2. Crush the petals in a mortar before adding them to the oil. Mix well and let cool.
3. Store the oil in a cool, dark place, but not in the refrigerator. Filter before each use.

Fresh petals can occasionally be added. Hildegard suggests heating the oil in a pan but also mentions the possibility of leaving it in the sun, as with the St. John's wort oil.

ಌ St. John's Wort Oil

Used to soothe mild burns and heal wounds. For any burn, immediately and thoroughly rinse with lukewarm (*not cold*) water.

Ingredients

- Fresh St. John's wort flowers, stems, and leaves
- Olive oil

Preparation

1. Fill a wide-necked glass bottle with St. John's wort flowers, stems, and (preferably) leaves, without overpacking. Top with olive oil.
2. Leave the bottle in the sun for about ten days, shaking occasionally.

The oil is ready when it turns red. Store in a corked bottle for year-round use.

ಌ Horseradish Powder

"When the horseradish is green, let it dry in the sun. Grind it into powder and add an equal weight of galangal. If suffering from heart problems, eat this powder on bread, either after a meal or on an empty stomach."

Hildegard also recommends horseradish powder in tea or warm wine for pulmonary infections (bronchitis, cough, etc.).

Ingredients

- 1 horseradish root

Preparation

1. Clean the root and cut it into thin slices.
2. Dry the slices in the open air, on a clean cloth, under the sun for at least one month.
3. Grind into a fine powder using a coffee or spice grinder.

❧ Wine Plaster

Caution: For skin ulcers, consult a doctor before applying anything to open lesions.

Ingredients

- ½ cup (10 cl) of red wine
- ½ cup (10 cl) of olive oil

Preparation

1. Mix the two liquids while heating gently with a wooden spoon, without boiling.
2. Turn off the heat, let cool slightly, and continue stirring.
3. Soak a cloth in the mixture and apply it to the affected area for about an hour. Repeat two to three times daily.

❧ Rye Poultice for Itching

Ingredients

- Crust of rye bread (or stale rye bread)
- Olive oil

Preparation

1. In a saucepan, mix the bread crust with olive oil to form a paste.
2. Heat gently, stirring continuously.

Apply the warm paste as a poultice. Repeat for three days, rinsing and rubbing each time with olive oil.

✷ Calendula Lotion (for the Skin and Hair)

Ingredients
- 1.75 oz (50 g) of fresh calendula flowers, or 1 oz (30 g) of roots
- 4 cups (1 liter) of water

Preparation
1. Soak the flowers or roots in cold water for 10 minutes.
2. Heat gently until boiling. For flowers, simmer for 1 minute; for roots, boil for 3 to 5 minutes.
3. Let cool, strain, and use as a rinse for hair.

For small skin lesions (eczema, scarred pimples, etc.), soak a cloth in the lotion and apply it to the affected area for 30 minutes.

Kitchen Recipes

Hildegard did not necessarily distinguish between a decoction of leaves and a vegetable soup. Indeed, the difference is subtle! To simplify, one could say that decoctions are typically made from dried plants, while soups are prepared with fresh plants. In this transformation, any edible plant transitions from being a "simple" to a "vegetable."

Often, vegetable soups (and medicinal plants) are enriched with meat broths. Porridges are thickened using wheat or spelt flour. However, Hildegard also offers several more elaborate recipes!

The following recipes are designed for four servings. In the case of porridges, soups, or purees, the number of diners is not specified — if there is too much, simply place the covered container in the refrigerator.

Fennel and Chervil Porridge

"Against the bad humors of the stomach, take fennel, slightly more nettle than fennel, and twice as much lovage as these two plants. Prepare a dish by adding flour or bread. Eat often."

Ingredients

- 3.5 oz (100 g) of fresh fennel (roots or leaves)
- 5.3 oz (150 g) of fresh nettle
- 17.5 oz (500 g) of chervil leaves (or mountain lovage)
- Stale bread

Preparation

1. Cook the fennel and chervil in water, adding the nettle at the end of the cooking process.
2. Drain using a slotted spoon and blend the mixture using a food mill.
3. Add the bread to thicken, crushing it coarsely.

As Hildegard suggests, fennel can be replaced with mallow, which likely has superior emollient properties.

Chamomile Porridge

"If you have stomach pain or when women have their menstruation, they should also eat this porridge."

Ingredients

- 3.5 oz (100 g) of fresh chamomile
- ¾ cup (70 g) of spelt flour
- ¾ cup + 1 tbsp (20 cl) of olive oil
- 1 cup (¼ liter) of water
- Salt, pepper (and optionally galangal, as Hildegard would appreciate!)

Preparation

1. Cook the chamomile in water without bringing it to a boil.
2. Blend to create a soup-like consistency.
3. Add the olive oil.
4. Gradually mix in the flour to thicken the porridge.
5. Season with salt and pepper.

Enjoy warm.

# Nutmeg and Gladiolus Porridge

"In case of cerebral paralysis, which may be linked to hemiplegia or a state of deep depression, give this to the patient twice daily until recovery."

Ingredients

- ½ nutmeg
- 1 tsp (5 g) of galangal
- 3.5 oz (100 g) of gladiolus root
- 7 oz (200 g) of plantain
- Stale bread
- Salt

Preparation

1. Grind the nutmeg into a powder.
2. In a saucepan, cook the finely chopped gladiolus root and plantain in a small amount of water over low heat.
3. Add the spices and salt, tasting to adjust the seasoning.
4. At the end of cooking, depending on the desired consistency, add stale bread to thicken.

Gladiolus has a bland taste, so the addition of nutmeg and galangal is quite helpful. Fennel can also be added to make the dish more appealing.

# Lupin Mash

"When you have a stomachache and suffer from bloating."

Ingredients

- 9 oz (250 g) of lupin seeds
- 7 oz (200 g) of stale bread, preferably spelt
- 1.75 oz (50 g) of fennel seeds
- 3.5 oz (100 g) of celery stalks (or marsh lovage)
- A pinch of baking soda
- Olive oil or butter

Preparation

1. Cook the lupin seeds in water or steam them together with the fennel seeds. Add a pinch of baking soda during cooking.
2. Blend the celery leaves into a paste.
3. Crush the stale bread into crumbs.
4. Once the lupin seeds are cooked, drain the water, and mix in the celery and bread.
5. Cook the mixture over low heat, adding a knob of butter or a spoonful of olive oil.
6. Mash everything into a purée.

The skin of lupins is bitter and can either be peeled or left on, depending on preference. A pinch of rosemary can be added to the cooking water to enhance the flavor.

Pear Compote with Chervil

"This preparation is a remedy more precious than gold and more useful than the purest gold. It eliminates migraines, removes bad humors, and purifies a person as one cleans a vase of the dirt it contains."

Ingredients (Serves 4)

- 2 pears (7 to 9 oz (200 to 250 g))
- 1 tbsp (20 g) of honey
- 3.5 oz (100 g) of chervil roots or fennel
- 1.75 oz (50 g) of ginger rhizomes
- 2 tsp to 1 tbsp (8 to 10 g) of fresh summer savory, or ½ to 1 tsp (3 to 5 g) dried (can be replaced with thyme)
- ½ to 1 tsp (3 to 5 g) of galangal
- 1 tsp (5 g) of licorice powder

Preparation

1. Chop the ginger, chervil roots, and pears into small pieces.
2. Begin by cooking the ginger and licorice in 2 cups (50 cl) of water for 10 minutes to soften them.
3. Add the pears and chervil roots. Occasionally remove excess water and set it aside. Let the mixture reduce until the pears can be mashed with a wooden spoon.
4. Heat the reserved water to steep the summer savory infusion.
5. At the end of cooking, pour the infused savory water into the mixture.
6. Stir well and pass the mixture through a food mill.
7. Add the galangal and licorice powder.
8. Mix the honey into the warm purée, adjusting the sweetness to taste.

Consume 1 tablespoon in the morning and evening. Fresh chervil leaves and fresh licorice root (softened with the ginger) can be used instead of dried forms. Keep the remedy in a sealed jar and refrigerate.

This remedy is not recommended for individuals with hypertension or those on corticosteroids.

Chestnuts with Sage Butter

Ingredients (Serves 4)

- 17.5 oz (500 g) of chestnuts
- 3 tbsp (40 g) of high-quality salted butter
- 3.5 oz (100 g) of fresh sage leaves
- Salt, pepper, galangal

Preparation

1. Make a small incision on the side of each chestnut, then place them in a pot of cold water.
2. Bring the water to a boil and cook for about 5 minutes.
3. Remove the shells and the brown inner skin.
4. Boil the peeled chestnuts in a second pot of boiling water for 20 minutes.
5. Drain and set aside.
6. In a frying pan, melt the butter over very low heat. Add the sage leaves and cook for no more than 2 minutes. Season with salt, pepper, and galangal.
7. Add the chestnuts to the pan and cook for 2 to 3 minutes.

The sage butter can also be used to season root vegetables (e.g., horseradish, potatoes, carrots) or as a complement to meat or fish dishes.

Fresh chestnuts are shiny and should feel full when pressed between your fingers. There should be no gap between the fruit and its shell. Ensure there are no holes in the shells, as these indicate the presence of insects or worms. To confirm their quality, place the chestnuts in a pot of cold water. Discard any that float and keep only those that sink — they are full and ready for cooking.

Green Soup

Ingredients

- 7 oz (200 g) of purslane
- 1.75 oz (50 g) of basil
- 3.5 oz (100 g) of aloe vera pulp
- Meat broth
- 3 medium potatoes
- 1 onion

Preparation

1. Cut the potatoes (unknown in Hildegard's time) and aloe vera (which Hildegard highly valued) into small pieces.
2. Cover with water and simmer.
3. Add the meat broth.
4. Meanwhile, sauté the sliced onion.
5. Add the purslane and mix everything together.
6. At the end of cooking, add the basil, salt, and pepper.

Celery Velouté with Hazelnuts

Ingredients

- 1 celery root
- ½ onion
- 5½ cups (1.3 liters) of water
- 1½ cup (30 cl) of fresh cream
- A dozen hazelnuts
- Salt, pepper

Preparation

1. Wash, peel, and dice the celery root.
2. Peel the onion.
3. Steam the celery root and onion, adding salt and pepper.
4. Toast the hazelnuts in a pan and crush them.
5. Blend the vegetables finely.
6. Add the cream and mix well.
7. Garnish with the crushed hazelnuts before serving.

Lentil Soup

Ingredients (Serves 4)

- 7 oz (200 g) of lentils
- 10.5 oz (300 g) of carrots
- Meat broth (homemade or pre-prepared)
- 1 large onion
- Olive oil

Preparation

1. In a pot, heat olive oil and sauté the sliced onions and carrot rounds.
2. Add the lentils and meat broth.
3. Cover with water and cook according to the type of lentil (red, green, etc.).
4. Once cooked, season to taste.
5. Let simmer on low heat for an additional 5 minutes.
6. Blend the soup if desired.
7. Optionally, stir in a spoonful of fresh cream or soy cream before serving.

Optional Variations

- Add 7 oz (200 g) of diced pumpkin at the same time as the lentils.
- Add 2 or 3 peeled tomatoes at the end of cooking.

Note: Pumpkin and tomatoes were unknown in Europe during Hildegard's time.

> *Like spelt, lentils appeared during the Neolithic period. They are among the earliest cultivated plants in human history, with their domestication coinciding with the birth of agriculture. Together, lentils and spelt enabled Homo sapiens to transition from hunter-gatherers to farmers, ensuring their survival through regular harvests.*

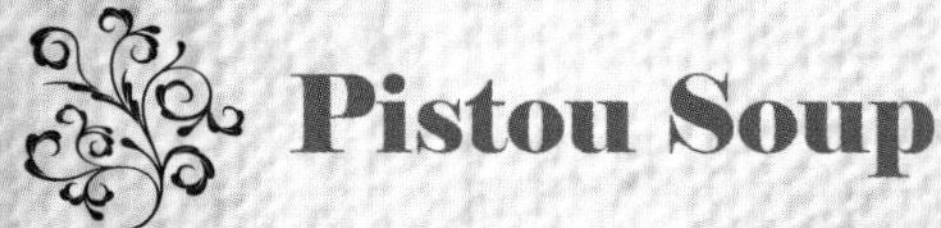

Pistou Soup

Tomatoes and eggplants were only introduced to Europe after the discovery of the Americas. Nonetheless, it would be a shame to overlook this delicious recipe, which also uses fava beans, carrots, basil, onion, and garlic, all praised by Hildegard.

Ingredients (Serves 4)

- 6 cups (1.5 liters) of water
- 4 small tomatoes
- 4.25 oz (120 g) of fresh fava beans
- 1 eggplant
- 3 carrots
- ¼ head of broccoli
- 1 onion
- 2 cloves of garlic
- 1 large handful of basil
- 5 tbsp of virgin olive oil
- 1 pinch of dried seaweed

Preparation

1. In olive oil, sauté the diced eggplant, sliced carrots, broccoli, peeled tomatoes, and onion.
2. Toss the fava beans and the sautéed vegetables into a pot of boiling water.
3. Meanwhile, prepare the pistou by crushing the basil and garlic in a mortar with a drizzle of olive oil.
4. After 5 minutes of cooking, stir the pistou into the vegetables. Salt as needed (possibly using baking soda).
5. Cook for another 5 minutes.

Tomatoes are native to Central and South America. The Aztecs cultivated them and prepared a sauce (or soup) combining tomatoes with chili and pumpkin seeds. In 1519, Hernán Cortés and the Spanish conquistadors discovered the tomato and brought it back to Europe.

Horseradish Frittata

Rafano is Italian for horseradish — hence, this rafano that is served for Mardi Gras. Except for the potato, which only appeared in Europe in the sixteenth century, all these ingredients are among the health foods that Hildegard recommended.

Ingredients (Serves 4)

- 8 eggs
- 7 oz (200 g) of horseradish root
- 14 oz (400 g) of potatoes
- 7 oz (200 g) of breadcrumbs
- 3.5 oz (100 g) of sausage (soppressata or chorizo)
- 3.5 oz (100 g) of grated Parmesan cheese (or Canestrato or Pecorino)
- Salt, pepper, olive oil

Preparation

1. Peel the potatoes and boil them in a pot of water.
2. Grate the horseradish.
3. Crack the eggs and beat them in a large bowl.
4. Drain the potatoes and mash them with a vegetable mill.
5. Mix the eggs with the mashed potatoes, then add the horseradish.
6. Incorporate the sausage and cheese, chopped into small pieces, as well as the breadcrumbs.
7. Pour olive oil into a cast-iron skillet or tart pan, then pour in the frittata mixture.
8. Bake in the oven at mid-level for 20 to 40 minutes, depending on the thickness of the frittata. Cover with parchment paper if needed.

Laurel and Almond Cookies

Ingredients (Serves 4)

- 1¼ cup plus 1 tbsp (150 g) of semi-wholemeal flour
- 3 tbsp (30 g) of bay leaf powder
- ½ cup (50 g) of almond flour
- 1 to 2 tbsp milk
- 1 stick plus 1 tbsp (125 g) of butter
- ⅔ cup (70 g) of organic powdered sugar
- ½ tsp (3 g) of ground cinnamon
- 1 to 1 ½ tsp (5 to 7 g) of ground ginger
- 1 to 1 ½ tsp (5 to 7 g) of ground dill
- ½ tsp (1 to 2 g) of ground cloves
- 1 tiny pinch (1 g) of galangal
- Salt

Preparation

1. Mix the dry ingredients together.
2. Add the milk and butter.
3. Knead until you get a smooth, non-sticky dough (adjust with milk if needed).
4. Using a piping bag or your fingers, form small dough strips.
5. Flatten and prick with a fork.
6. Bake at 320°F for 8 to 10 minutes (the biscuits should barely brown).
7. Let cool on the tray, then fully cool.

Enjoy immediately—or lock up to keep yourself from overindulging.

Oatcakes

Ingredients

- 1¾ cups (200 g) of rolled oats
- 2 cups (½ liter) of milk
- 2 eggs
- Nutmeg
- 3.5 oz (100 g) of aged Crottin de Chavignol cheese, grated
- Salt

Preparation

1. Soak the oats in milk for 30 minutes. Drain.
2. Beat the eggs, add nutmeg and salt.
3. Mix everything together and form small patties. Flatten them. Place them on a baking tray.
4. Sprinkle with cheese. Bake until golden, about 15 minutes.

Limonia (Lemon Chicken)

Ingredients

- 1 chicken
- 5.3 oz (150 g) of bacon lardons
- 2 onions
- 2 untreated lemons
- 1½ cups (150 g) of almond flour
- 1 tsp of ground ginger
- ½ tsp of ground nutmeg
- 3 cloves, ground
- 2 cups (50 cl) of chicken stock
- 1 egg yolk
- Olive oil
- Salt
- Long pepper (or black pepper)

Preparation

1. In a Dutch oven or heavy pot, heat the olive oil and sauté the sliced onions and lardons. Set them aside. If needed, add more olive oil to the pot and brown the chicken.
2. While the chicken browns, prepare the chicken stock. Stir the almond flour into the stock and whisk for about 10 minutes. Strain the mixture.
3. Once the chicken is golden, return the onions and lardons to the pot. Add the almond-infused stock, ginger, nutmeg, ground cloves, pepper, and salt. Cover and simmer for 45 minutes.
4. Add the lemons, cut into pieces with the zest, and continue cooking covered for an additional 10 minutes.

This dish is inspired by a recipe from the *Liber de Coquina* (fourteenth century), translated below:

> "Chicken with lemon: To make chicken with lemon, fry the chicken with lard and onions. Blanch almonds, grind them, dilute with meat stock, and strain. Cook this with the chicken and spices. If almonds are not available, the stock may be thickened with egg yolks. When it is time to serve, add the juice of lemon, lime, or bitter orange."

# Pesto

Ingredients

- 1.75 oz (50 g) of fresh basil leaves
- 1.75 oz (50 g) of grated Parmesan cheese
- ⅓ cup (30 g) of almond flour
- 2 garlic cloves
- ½ cup plus 1 tbsp olive oil
- 1 tbsp lemon juice
- Salt and pepper

Preparation

1. Peel the garlic cloves, cut them in half, and remove the germ.
2. Blend the basil and garlic.
3. Add the Parmesan, olive oil, lemon juice, and almond flour, then blend for a few more seconds.
4. Season with salt and pepper to taste.

> It is likely that Hildegard was familiar with Parmesan cheese, as this pressed cheese dates back to the eleventh century. Invented by monks in Lombardy, Parmesan is made from cow's milk that has been partially skimmed by surface skimming. It was formed into large wheels, and its reputation quickly spread, leading to imitations throughout northern Italy and even Switzerland.

Honey-Filled Iris Rhizomes

Hildegard was wary of frenzy, nervous crises, or excessive excitement, often accompanied by tremors or palpitations. She observed that iris had a soothing effect. To combat nervousness, irritability, or insomnia, the following recipe can be consumed as a dessert or applied as a poultice. However, take care: while the dessert and poultice can be prepared simultaneously, you must never ingest a poultice that has already been used, nor reuse it. After ten to twenty minutes of application, the poultice must be discarded.

Ingredients

- 2 to 3 large iris rhizomes per person
- ¼ to ½ cup (100 to 200 g) of honey

Preparation

1. Peel the rhizomes. Place them in simmering water (or steam them).
2. Once cooked (similar to a potato) and hot, cut into them, removing any fibrous parts.
3. Add honey and bake at a moderate temperature for 15 to 20 minutes.

Hildegard also provides a variation of this recipe: "Slice the iris into rounds, soften them with honey, and feed them to the person suffering from frenzy." The dish (or remedy) can be enjoyed hot or cold. For the poultice: Mash the mixture into a paste and apply it while warm, but not burning, to the chest, forehead, or thighs.

BIBLIOGRAPHY

Bézanger, L., Beauquesne, M. Pinkas, and M. Tork. *Les plantes dans la thérapeutique moderne.* Paris: Éditions Maloine, 1986.

Blimoff, Michèle. *Promenades dans des jardins disparus: Les plantes au Moyen Âge d'après les Grandes Heures d'Anne de Bretagne.* Rennes: Éditions Ouest-France, 2001.

Boulard, Bernard. *Dictionnaire des plantes médicinales du monde.* Paris: Éditions Estem, 2001.

Bruneton, Jean. *Éléments de phytochimie et de pharmacognosie.* Paris: Techniques et Documentation, 1987.

Ferris, Paul. *Les remèdes de santé de Hildegarde de Bingen.* Paris: Éditions Marabout, 2002, 2009, 2019.

Ferris, Paul. *J'aime les mauvaises herbes.* Paris: Éditions Marabout, 2019.

Fournier, Abbé P. *Le livre des plantes médicinales et vénéneuses de France, tomes I à III.* Paris: Éditions Lechevallier, 1947.

Guguenheim, Sylvain. *La Sybille du Rhin.* Paris: Publication de la Sorbonne, 1996.

Hildegard de Bingen. *Causes et remèdes.* Translated by Pierre Monat. Grenoble: Éditions Jérôme Millon, 1997.

Hildegard de Bingen. *Le livre des subtilités des créatures divines de diverses natures, tomes I and III.* Translated by Pierre Monat. Grenoble: Éditions Jérôme Millon, 1996.

Hildegard de Bingen. *Le livre des subtilités des créatures de diverses natures, tomes I and II.* Translated by Bernard Verten. Paris: Éditions Grégoriennes, 2013.

Hildegard de Bingen. *Scivias. Connaissez les Voies du Seigneur: L'intégrale des trois livres de visions et révélations.* Paris: Éditions Chamonal, 1909.

Hildegard de Bingen. *Scivias ou les trois livres, visions et révélations.* Paris: Princeps de l'édition Henri Étienne, Éditions Chamonal, 1912.

Hildegard de Bingen. *Scrivias ou "Sache les voies": Les livres des visions.* Translated by Pierre Monat. Paris: Éditions du Cerf, 1996.

Moulinier, Laurence. *Le manuscrit perdu de Strasbourg.* Paris: Publication de la Sorbonne, 1995.

Moulinier, Laurence. *Plantes toxiques et humeurs peccantes: La pensée du poison dans l'œuvre de Hildegarde.* In *Le corps à l'épreuve. Poisons, remèdes et chirurgie: Aspects des pratiques médicales dans l'Antiquité et au Moyen Âge,* edited by HAL archives. HAL Archives, 1999.

Moulinier, Laurence. *Hildegard de Bingen: Les plantes médicinales et le jugement de la postérité.* HAL, 1993.

Pernoud, Régine. *Hildegarde de Bingen.* Paris: Le Livre de poche, 1994.

Strehlow, Wighard. *Hildegarde de Bingen: Prévention et guérison des maladies.* Paris: Éditions Dangles, 1997.

Strehlow, Wighard. *Guérir par l'alimentation selon Hildegarde de Bingen.* Paris: Éditions du Rocher, 2019.

Strehlow, Wighard. *La guérison du corps et de l'esprit selon Hildegarde de Bingen.* Paris: Éditions Dangles, 2002.

Strehlow, Wighard. *Prévention et guérison selon Hildegarde de Bingen.* Paris: Éditions du Rocher, 2020.

Thomas, Elisabeth. *Hildegard von Bingen: Chants de l'extase.* Hamburg: Deutsche Harmonia Mundi, 1994.

Vannier, Marie-Anne. *Les visions d'Hildegarde de Bingen.* Paris: Albin Michel, 2015.

Wichtl, M., and R. Anton. *Plantes thérapeutiques.* Paris: Éditions Technique & Documentation, Éditions Médicales Internationales, 1999.

INDEX

Plants by Latin Name

Remedies

Recipes

Image Credits

Illumination from Hildegard's *Scivias*, 1151, public domain / commons.wikimedia.org

Illumination from Hildegard's *Scivias*, 1151, public domain / commons.wikimedia.org

Calendar of Seasons, Wien, ÖNB, *Codex 387*, fol. 90v, public domain / www.loc.gov/item/2021667978

Map, J. Ch. Joannis, Disibodenberg Monastery Ruins, 1724, public domain

Melencolia I, 1514 engraving by Albrecht Dürer, public domain / commons.wikimedia.org

Brewers, Amman, *Das Ständebuch* (The Book of Trades), 1568, public domain / commons.wikimedia.org

Antiphon, Folium 466 recto do *Riesencodex*, 1175/1190, public domain / commons.wikimedia.org

Agrimonia eupatoria, Woodville, *Medical Botany*, Vol 2, plate 180, public domain / Wellcomecollection.org

Allium sativum, Woodville, *Medical Botany*, Vol 4, plate 25, public domain / Wellcomecollection.org

Aloe vera, Candolle, *Plantarum historia succulentarum*, 1802, public domain / commons.wikimedia.org

Prunus amygdalus, Köhler, *Medizinal-Pflanzen*, vol 2, 1897, public domain

Anethum graveolens, Woodville, *Medical Botany*, plate 48, public domain / Wellcomecollection.org

Angelica archangelica, Köhler, *Medizinal-Pflanzen*, vol 2, 1897, public domain

Avena sativa, Host, *Icones et descriptiones Graminum austriacorum*, 1801, public domain / commons.wikimedia.org

Arctium lappa, Woodville, *Medical Botany*, Vol 1, plate 13, public domain / Wellcomecollection.org

Ocimum basilicum, Dietrich, *Flora medica*, Pl. 135, 1828, public domain / commons.wikimedia.org

Buxus sempervireus, Thomé, *Flora von Deutschland, Österreich und der Schweiz*, 1885, Gera, Germany, public domain / commons.wikimedia.org

Chrysanthemum parthenium, Woodville, *Medical Botany*, vol 1, plate 30, public domain / Wellcomecollection.org

Cinnamomum, Spices, their nature and growth, the vanilla bean, a talk on tea, Baltimore, Md., McCormick & co: 1915. public domain / commons.wikimedia.org

Daucus carota, Baxter, *British Phaenogamous Botany*, 1834, public domain

Apium graveolens, Thomé, *Flora von Deutschland, Österreich und der Schweiz* 1885, Gera, Germany, public domain / commons.wikimedia.org

Anthriscus silvestris, Köhler, *Medizinal-Pflanzen*, Vol 3, plate 37, public domain / commons.wikimedia.org

Centaurea benedicta, Köhler, *Medizinal-Pflanzen*, 1887, public domain / commons.wikimedia.org

Castanea sativa, (214588292), Mannaggia / stock.adobe.com

Brassica oleracea, Plantarum indigenarum et exoticarum icones ad vivum coloratae, 1792, public domain / commons.wikimedia.org

Cydonia oblonga, Köhler, *Medizinal-Pflanzen*, vol 1, 1897, public domain

Cuminum cyminum, Köhler, *Medizinal-Pflanzen*, vol 3, 1897, public domain

Triticum spelta, Host, *Icones et descriptiones Graminum austriacorum*, 1801, public domain / commons.wikimedia.org

Foeniculum vulgare, Köhler, *Medizinal-Pflanzen*, vol 2, 1897, public domain

Vicia faba, Thomé, *Flora von Deutschland, Österreich und der Schweiz* 1885, Gera, Germany, public domain / commons.wikimedia.org

Dryopteris filix, Köhler, *Medizinal-Pflanzen*, 1887, public domain / commons.wikimedia.org

Gentiana lutea, Köhler, *Medizinal-Pflanzen*, vol 4, 1897, public domain

Zingiber officinale, Woodville, *Medical Botany*, Vol 4, plate 250, public domain / Wellcomecollection.org

Humulus, Thomé, *Flora von Deutschland, Österreich und der Schweiz* 1885, Gera, Germany, public domain / commons.wikimedia.org

Iris germanica, Thomé, *Flora von Deutschland, Österreich und der Schweiz* 1885, Gera, Germany, public domain / commons.wikimedia.org

Laurus nobilis, Thomé, *Flora von Deutschland, Österreich und der Schweiz* 1885, Gera, Germany, public domain / commons.wikimedia.org

Lavandula officinalis, Köhler, *Medizinal-Pflanzen*, vol 1, 1897, public domain

Lens culinaris, Thomé, *Flora von Deutschland, Österreich und der Schweiz* 1885, Gera, Germany, public domain / commons.wikimedia.org

Lupinus albus, Turpin, *Flore Médicale 4*, plate 223, 1834, public domain / commons.wikimedia.org

Malva sylvestris, Köhler, *Medizinal-Pflanzen*, vol 1, 1897, public domain

Cucumis melo, (176702443), © Mannaggia / public domain / stock.adobe.com

Mentha piperita, Köhler, *Medizinal-Pflanzen*, vol 1, 1897, public domain

Hypericum perforatum, Fitschen, *Pflanzen der Heimat*, 1913, public domain / commons.wikimedia.org

Myristica fragrans, Köhler, *Medizinal-Pflanzen*, vol 2, 1897, public domain

Ordeum vulgare, Zorn, *Afbeeldingen*, Vol 6, plate 536, public domain / babel.hathitrust.org

Urtica dioica, Thomé, *Flora von Deutschland, Österreich und der Schweiz* 1885, Gera, Germany, public domain / commons.wikimedia.org

Rumex acetosa, Zorn, *Afbeeldingen*, Vol 2, plate 145, public domain / babel.hathitrust.org

Petroselinum hortense, Thomé, *Flora von Deutschland, Österreich und der Schweiz* 1885, Gera, Germany, public domain / commons.wikimedia.org

Taraxacum officinale, Köhler, *Medizinal-Pflanzen*, vol 1, 1897, public domain

Plantago major, Plantago media or *Plantago lanceolata*, Siélain, *Atlas de Poche des Plantes des Champs, des Prairies et des Bois*, 1895, public domain / commons.wikimedia.org

Allium ampeloprasum, Antique Chromo-Lithograph, 1880, public domain

Pyrus communis, (238750693) © Rey Kamensky / stock.adobe.com

Pisum sativum, Thomé, *Flora von Deutschland, Österreich und der Schweiz* 1885, Gera, Germany, public domain / commons.wikimedia.org

Cicer arietinum, 1772, public domain / commons.wikimedia.org

Malus domestica or *Malus sieversii*, Köhler, *Medizinal-Pflanzen*, vol, 1897, public domain

Portulaca oleracea, Thomé, *Flora von Deutschland, Österreich und der Schweiz* 1885, Gera, Germany, public domain / commons.wikimedia.org

Pulmonaria officinalis, Lindman, *Bilder ur Nordens Flora*, 1926, public domain / commons.wikimedia.org

Armoracia rusticana, Kop, *Flora Batava*, Volume 4, 1822, public domain / commons.wikimedia.org

Salvia rosmarinus or *Rosmarinus officinalis*, Köhler, *Medizinal-Pflanzen*, vol, 1897, public domain

Rubus fruticosus, U.S. Department of Agriculture Pomological Watercolor Collection by Deborah Griscom Passmore (1840-1911), public domain / commons.wikimedia.org

Rosa gallica, Pierre-Joseph Redouté, 1824, public domain / commons.wikimedia.org

Salvia officinalis, Köhler, *Medizinal-Pflanzen*, vol 1, 1897, public domain

Calendula arvensis, Köhler, *Medizinal-Pflanzen*, vol 3, 1897, public domain

Thymus vulgaris, Köhler, *Medizinal-Pflanzen*, vol, 1897, public domain

Tilia platyphyllos, Pierre-Joseph Redouté, public domain / commons.wikimedia.org

Valeriana officinalis, *Billeder af Nordens Flora*, Vol 1, plate 60, public domain / biodiversitylibrary.org

Viola odorata, (162322079) © Archivist / stock.adobe.com

The Vendanges, from a tract on Winemaking by Arnaldus de Villanova, translated to German by Wilhelm von Hirnkofen, 1506, public domain / commons.wikimedia.org

Line-art portrait of Hildegard of Bingen (1647836983), © Natata / Shutterstock.com

Background Texture (7232409), © Artem Podrez / Pexels.com

Background Texture (6485437), © Eva Bronzini / Pexels.com

Hand Drawn Botanical Pattern (14571241), designed by Freepik.com

Background Texture (6485422), © Eva Bronzini / Pexels.com

About the Author

French journalist Paul Ferris specializes in health and natural therapies. He is the author of numerous natural health guides and regularly appears on television and radio programs.

Sophia Institute

Sophia Institute is a nonprofit institution that seeks to nurture the spiritual, moral, and cultural life of souls and to spread the gospel of Christ in conformity with the authentic teachings of the Roman Catholic Church.

Sophia Institute Press fulfills this mission by offering translations, reprints, and new publications that afford readers a rich source of the enduring wisdom of mankind.

Sophia Institute also operates the popular online resource CatholicExchange.com. *Catholic Exchange* provides world news from a Catholic perspective as well as daily devotionals and articles that will help readers to grow in holiness and live a life consistent with the teachings of the Church.

In 2013, Sophia Institute launched Sophia Institute for Teachers to renew and rebuild Catholic culture through service to Catholic education. With the goal of nurturing the spiritual, moral, and cultural life of souls, and an abiding respect for the role and work of teachers, we strive to provide materials and programs that are at once enlightening to the mind and ennobling to the heart; faithful and complete, as well as useful and practical.

Sophia Institute gratefully recognizes the Solidarity Association for preserving and encouraging the growth of our apostolate over the course of many years. Without their generous and timely support, this book would not be in your hands.

www.SophiaInstitute.com
www.CatholicExchange.com
www.SophiaTeachers.org

Sophia Institute Press is a registered trademark of Sophia Institute.
Sophia Institute is a tax-exempt institution as defined by the
Internal Revenue Code, Section 501(c)(3). Tax ID 22-2548708.

"Like billowing clouds,
Like the incessant
gurgle of the brook,
The longing of the spirit
can never be stilled."

ST. HILDEGARD

St. Hildegard's Garden

Paul Ferris

ISBN: 979-8-88911-372-0

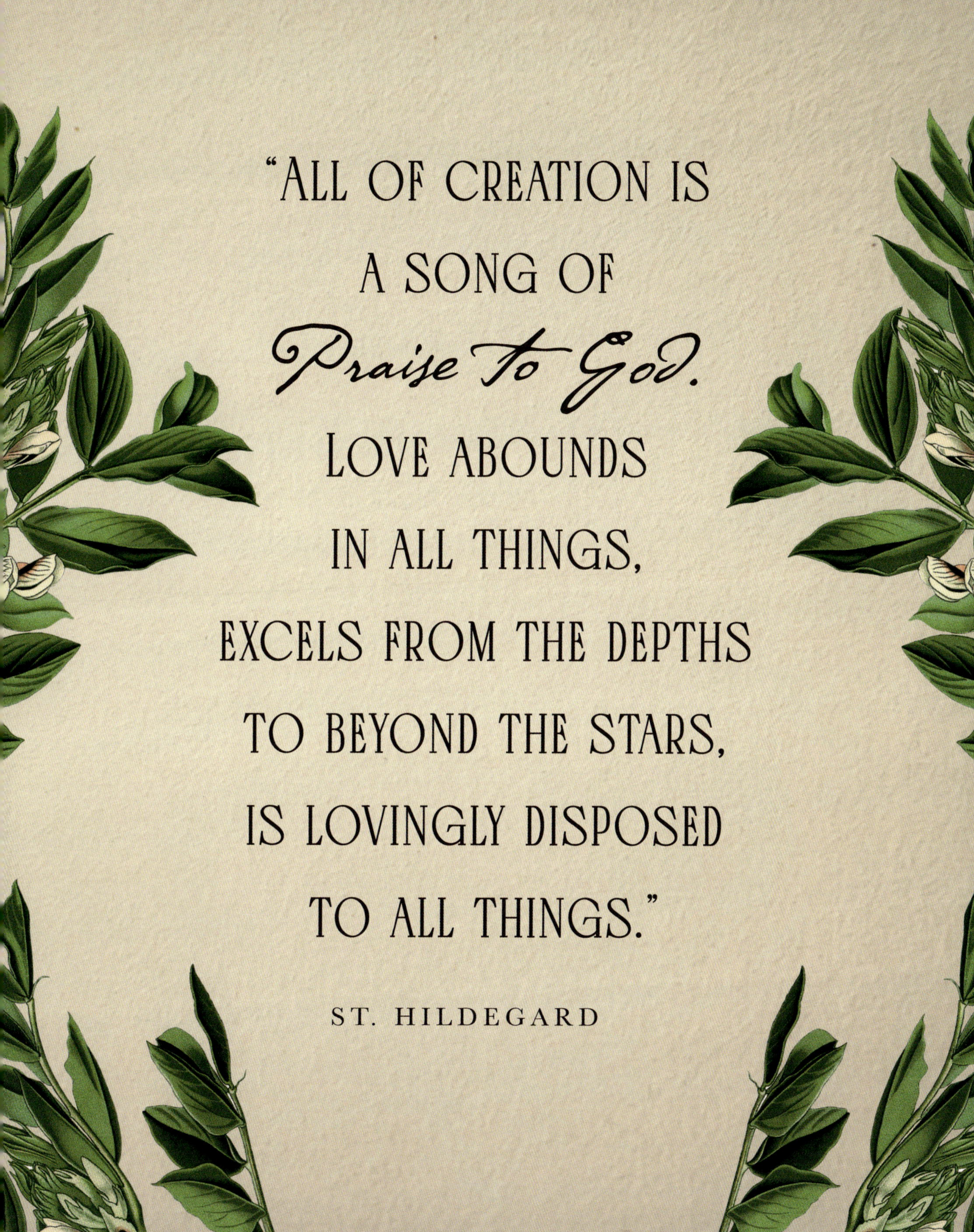

"ALL OF CREATION IS
A SONG OF
Praise to God.
LOVE ABOUNDS
IN ALL THINGS,
EXCELS FROM THE DEPTHS
TO BEYOND THE STARS,
IS LOVINGLY DISPOSED
TO ALL THINGS."
ST. HILDEGARD

St. Hildegard's Garden

Paul Ferris

SOPHIA
INSTITUTE PRESS
www.SophiaInstitute.com

ISBN: 979-8-88911-372-0

Rosa Gallica flore gigantea.   *Rosier* de Provins à fleur gigantesque.

P.J. Redouté pinx.   Imprimerie de Remond   Victor sculp

St. Hildegard's Garden

Paul Ferris

On the other side: *Rosa gallica flore giganteo*, a painted engraving
of a rose by Pierre-Joseph Redouté, 1824.

SOPHIA
INSTITUTE PRESS

www.SophiaInstitute.com

ISBN: 979-8-88911-372-0

335. *Buxus sempervirens* L. Immergrüner Buchsbaum.

St. Hildegard's Garden

Paul Ferris

On the other side: Buxus sempervirens from Prof. Dr. Otto Wilhelm Thomé's Flora von Deutschland, Österreich und der Schweiz, 1885, Gera, Germany.

SOPHIA
INSTITUTE PRESS

www.SophiaInstitute.com

ISBN: 979-8-88911-372-0